the WEDDING *Roller Coaster*

Keeping Your Relationships Intact Through the Ups and Downs

LEAH WEINBERG

The WEDDING *Roller Coaster*

Copyright © 2021 by Color Pop Publishing, LLC - *First Edition*

ColorPopEvents.com

ISBN: 978-0-578-88301-4

eBook: 978-0-578-88302-1

Cover & *interior design by Gregory Rohm*

Printed in the United States of America

FOLLOW ME ON SOCIAL MEDIA

@colorpopevents

Get to Know Leah Weinberg

Unflappable. Calm under (extreme) pressure.
Keeps her cool—with her sense of humor intact.

This is how clients described Color Pop Events founder Leah Weinberg during her former career as a commercial real estate attorney. Today, happy couples have come to rely on that same soothing confidence and rock-solid competence when planning their wedding.

Early in her legal career, it became clear to Leah that she was destined to be her own boss. Constantly brainstorming business ideas, it wasn't until she planned her own wedding in 2012—dubbed the "wedding of the year" by multiple guests—that she knew she'd found her calling. Wedding planning combined her passion for spreadsheets with her love of seeing people relax, smile and laugh. In 2013, Leah launched Color Pop Events to bring her eye for detail and flawless event execution to couples in and around New York City.

Leah applies an attorney's meticulousness to all weddings. She forecasts multiple steps ahead of the game, navigating complexities and steering clear of (or quickly resolving) any problems with limitless energy and resourcefulness.

Whether your wedding is brash and bold or sweet and intimate, Leah turns overwhelming into easy with a smile, serenity, and a contagious spirit that couples find wonderfully refreshing.

Each year, Color Pop Events is proud to donate a portion of its profits to charitable organizations like Project Q, Black Mamas Matter Alliance, Planned Parenthood, ACLU, and Animal Haven.

"A wedding is a celebration of you and your partner's love. The details like the napkin color and floral arrangements are wonderful, but they're not the most important thing. I realized that all that stuff is superfluous -- what made that day so incredible was being able to truly celebrate with our community. To this day, our friends tell us that it was the most fun and memorable wedding they had ever been to."

– Shirin Eskandani

TABLE *of* CONTENTS

Introduction

As I see it, there are two paths to take when planning a wedding. There's the "It's my day, I'm going to do it my way, screw everybody else" approach. And then there's the "It's my day, but I want to be thoughtful about what's happening with the people around me and preserving those relationships" approach. This book strives towards the latter line of thinking—because you'll have a much better experience. *Promise!*

When I started talking to people about the idea for this book, I explained that I wanted to write a book for engaged couples about the emotional side of wedding planning that would help them as individuals maintain healthy relationships with themselves, their partner, their family, and everyone else around them during the process.

As a wedding planner and former lawyer, I've seen it all first-hand. My approach to wedding planning is multi-faceted: On the one hand, it's very systematic and organized, but on the other hand, I lead with compassion, heart, and empathy. Building genuine relationships with my clients is a huge priority for me, and crafting a wedding that truly feels like them is even more important. I give my clients permission in the planning process to just be *themselves* and to throw tradition out the window if that's what they want. And I try to lead by example. I live my life vivaciously-out-loud. From Baby Yoda memes to rainbow *everything*, I embrace my outrageous love of color, quirkiness, creativity, and personal style—all at once. I want each one of my couples to do the same. Because what good is a wedding (and, frankly, life) if you can't be your true self?

So here we are: *the wedding roller coaster.* Through this book, I hope to hold your hand through the ups and downs of planning a wedding by preparing you for what you're about to encounter. This book will give you the tools to maintain your mental health and preserve healthy relationships in the planning process while helping you focus less on the stress and more on the outcome. You are getting married, after all!

I've divided this book into three parts:

 PART ONE focuses on the personal and the practical. In these chapters, you'll learn about the inner work and conversations that will help set you and your partner up for success in the wedding planning process. I also discuss some practical guidance for the early wedding planning to-do's you'll encounter: preparing a budget, creating a guest list, hiring your vendors, and figuring out how to craft a wedding that feels like the two of you.

 PART TWO leans into the mental, emotional, and physical. I'll discuss some of the emotions you may find yourself experiencing during wedding planning and do a deep dive into stress to understand the mental and physical effects it has on you.

 PART THREE is all about your relationships with people *other* than your partner. That's where you'll get some understanding and advice around relationships with your family, your wedding party (if you choose to have one), and your guests.

The relationships that you have with yourself and your partner are where you'll notice I spend the bulk of this book because those relationships will consume most of your time when wedding planning. And those relationships are truly the most important, *aren't they?*

Before we dive in, there are some overarching points I need you to remember:

1. I am not a psychiatrist, psychologist, therapist, physician, or other healthcare or medical practitioner. I am, however, a wedding planner, a writer, and an attorney. This book is not meant to help diagnose

conditions, be a substitute for professional care, or be used to contradict any advice provided by a professional. It is simply a somewhat academic and sometimes light-hearted approach to understanding the wild world of weddings.

2. It is not my intent that this book be used to judge people's behavior and label it as "good" or "bad." I'm not here to say whether people should or should not act a certain way. I'm just here to help identify common behaviors, suggest some underlying causes, and give people the tools to recognize and navigate those behaviors.

3. This book is about a thoughtful approach to wedding planning. While I believe that your wedding is your day and should reflect you and your partner, that doesn't mean that you have to say "buzz off" to everyone else. You can still make your wedding yours and maintain healthy relationships with those around you during the process.

4. My pronouns are she/her/hers, but I don't want to assume the pronouns of anyone reading this book, so I'll use "they/them/their" for individuals as much as possible to be gender non-specific. Also, this book is geared towards monogamous, two-partner relationships, but I do acknowledge that relationships are a spectrum, and not all relationships are monogamous or two-partner.

5. As a cisgender, heterosexual white woman, I acknowledge the privilege that I hold and that I cannot speak to everyone's experiences. Because I want this book to be for everyone, I've included real-life accounts from married folks as Been There, Done That notes. These contributors are not all cis, hetero white women and are people who have literally been there and done that when it comes to some of the situations I address in this book. I have also collaborated with individuals (where indicated) to tackle topics that are not appropriate for me to speak on alone.

6. Some of the stories and examples in this book are hypothetical, others were inspired by behavior I've seen first-hand, and some are accounts I've been privy to from other wedding vendors and friends. Most names have been changed unless I've gained permission from each couple or individual involved.

Now that that's out of the way, let's get started, shall we?

Part One:

Chapter 1:
Start with the Heart Work and Set Expectations

The first few steps make all the difference...

What You'll Learn:

- Asking the right questions up front can help create realistic expectations and start your planning process off right.

- Creating meaningful space in the wedding planning process and on your wedding day will help you savor the experience—instead of feeling rushed through it all.

- Reframing both your wedding day and expectations can relieve pressure, elevate the truly important moments, and decrease perfectionism. Your wedding is about what you want—not what anyone else says it should be.

It's safe to say that you've never experienced anything quite like the wedding planning process before (unless, of course, this isn't your first rodeo), and if the stories in this book are any indication, you are in for one wild ride. From all of the deep conversations you'll have to magnifying family dynamics to bizarre behavior from your guests, you're going to be traversing a lot of new territory. And one of the best tools to help you navigate this process with your mental health and relationships intact is the ability for you and your partner to consistently turn inwards to ground yourselves.

How to Set Yourself up for Success from the Beginning

At the start of wedding planning, before you start assembling a rough guest list or looking at venues or going down the Pinterest rabbit hole, take some time to first sit down with yourself, get curious, and ask yourself a handful of questions:

- What narratives, beliefs, and stories do I hold about relationships and marriage?
- What does marriage mean to me?
- Am I distinguishing the legal marriage from the wedding celebration?
- What does an ideal wedding celebration feel like?
- What emotions do I anticipate encountering during this process?
- What challenges might I face?

These questions are relevant and important because of the long-standing beliefs that society holds about what a relationship should look like, what a marriage should look like, and what a wedding should look like. There will be pressure around what you create, including who is supposed to be there with you and how it's supposed to look and feel. You need to acknowledge these standards and make a conscious decision of whether you want to play into those traditions or not.

As Jesse Kahn, LCSW-R, CST, an NYC-based psychotherapist and sex therapist (and the Founder and Director at The Gender & Sexuality Therapy Center), points out, weddings are often a show. And that might not feel right to you and your partner. He notes that a marriage ceremony is an extremely vulnerable and intimate moment, and partners should be aware that they are inviting a number of people into that space when they may not have vulnerable relationships with all or any of their guests. Again, it's so critical for you to really explore what you want so that you can craft a wedding that feels right and comfortable to you.

For this activity, it's ideal that both partners participate in the solo exercise and then have a conversation to share the answers. Once you've both been honest about past experiences, what marriage means to you, and the emotions you hope to have and expect to encounter during this process and on the wedding day, you will be able to address some of the more practical considerations of the wedding.

Questions I often ask couples to noodle on include:

- Do we care if it's a short or a long engagement?
- Are there underlying factors that would push us towards getting married sooner rather than later? For example, wanting to start a family, timing with school or a job, our health, the health of a family member, etc.
- Is there a particular season in which we'd like to get married?
- In what city will it take place?
- How many people will we invite?
- Do we want a venue that's indoors, outdoors, or a combination of both?
- What type of venue aesthetic feels like us?

This is why we ask questions up front, because if you're not on the same page about what the wedding celebration itself is going to look like, then it's time to have a much larger conversation. Consider taking time to talk through what each of you wants, why it's important, and how you can compromise in order to plan an event that is comfortable to you both and meets both of your needs. If one partner wants a wedding in their hometown (where you *don't* live) in a barn with 50 close family and friends and the other wants a wedding in Chicago (where you *do* live) in a raw, industrial space with 200 guests, then the two of you will have to work through that.

You'll have to narrow in on what's important to you and why it's important to you, and then get creative about how you can have a wedding that addresses both partners' must-haves. Communication and compromise will be key. Firstly, you need to make sure you and your partner are honest about why something is important and communicate that reasoning clearly. Secondly, like any relationship, there's going to have to be some give and take. If one partner needs to get married in their hometown so that specific

VIP guests can attend, maybe you compromise and go with the other partner's preference on the size of the wedding. Also, keep in mind that sometimes compromise can result in eloping or even having two events so that everyone's boxes can be checked.

Once you two are aligned about the emotions behind your marriage, the "why" of the wedding, and the basics of the look and feel, it's going to give you confidence in making decisions about your wedding, and it's going to help you craft a more meaningful event. You'll be able to stand your ground when people around you try to force their desires and expectations upon you. A unified approach allows you to respond that you are on the same page and have given it careful thought—*that's powerful!*

Know Your Emotional Priorities

From a practical standpoint, once you've done the exploration into the meaning behind your marriage and have a sense of how the wedding will look and feel, you should also take a minute to set your emotional priorities for the wedding day. As Shirin Eskandani, a mindset and mindfulness coach and founder of Whole Hearted Coaching, recommends, couples should establish the five core feelings they want to have on their wedding day and determine how to make that possible.

She outlines the following five-step process to make the exercise more achievable:

1. Think about what feelings you value when it comes to your everyday life and also your wedding.
2. Put pen to paper and create a list (from the feelings you identified in Step One) of specific words that make you feel alive.
3. Narrow that list down to five words (your five core values for your wedding day).
4. You and your partner need to share your lists.
5. Determine three small ways that each of you can facilitate those feelings on your wedding day.

 **PRO TIP:** If you have a wedding planner, let them know what your feelings are! It may seem a little vulnerable, but then your planner will know your guiding principles for your wedding day and do whatever they can to help you experience everything your heart desires.

Shirin also suggests that couples plan specific moments on their wedding day to stop, pause, and savor – intentionally take in what's happening around them – and appoint someone like a member of the wedding party, a family member, or a wedding planner to remind them to do this. A moment that stands out to me is when the couple sits down to dinner – it's the perfect chance to pause, observe, and note that all of your favorite people on the planet are in one room together.

As Shirin so wisely points out, things may not look or happen on your wedding day exactly the way you expect them to. But if things *feel* the way you want to feel, then that is a success!

Know Your EQ

Did you know that you and your partner might be differently equipped when it comes to how each of you handles the emotions of wedding planning? It's true. It's called emotional intelligence (EQ), and it might give you or your partner an advantage in navigating the stressors of the wedding planning process.

A person's level of emotional intelligence reflects how good they are at identifying, managing, and using their own emotions as well as identifying and managing the emotions of others. This may be easier for people who are very in touch with and mindful of their own emotions. For others, it can be difficult to damn-near impossible. EQ is vital when recognizing how to manage yourself, the situation, and others' feelings. It's one of the best tools to have when planning a wedding.

Author and Founder and Chair of the Center for Healthy Minds at the University of Wisconsin-Madison, Richard Davidson, takes EQ a step further with the idea of a person's "emotional style." Think of emotional style like someone being street smart (as opposed to book smart) when it comes to their emotions – it's about being able to identify what you're feeling and how to handle it. The six characteristics that determine your or your partner's emotional style are:

- **Resilience:** Your ability to bounce back after being faced with stress, problems, obstacles, and challenges.
- **Outlook:** Your ability to keep a positive or optimistic outlook on things.
- **Social intuition:** Your ability to read social cues and other people's emotions.
- **Self-awareness:** Your ability to connect physical feelings with your emotional feelings.
- **Sensitivity to context:** Your ability to use your environment to control (or not control) your emotions.
- **Attention:** Your ability to focus.

It might seem silly to rate yourself on each of these qualities, but knowing up front how good you are at handling the stress, anxiety, and roller coaster of emotions that come with planning a wedding (and more importantly, where your weaknesses lie) will help you and your partner handle wedding planning in an emotionally healthy way.

Richard Davidson also speaks about self-awareness, though the concept deserves a different lens in the context of wedding planning. While he focused on a person's ability to connect their physical sensations with what they were feeling emotionally, I want to spend a minute on self-awareness as it relates to being mindful and aware of your own behaviors. Being self-aware is a major component of a successful wedding planning experience and in maintaining healthy relationships with everyone around you during the wedding planning process.

One aspect of self-awareness is knowing how others perceive you. Frankly, you've got to be aware of how you're coming off to those around you to prevent eliciting negative responses from them. I had a couple who always joked that they must be my worst couple ever. But the fact that they felt like they were a burden to me and that they were difficult shows a level of self-awareness that actually made them NOT difficult. It's the ones who have no self-awareness of how they're behaving that are actually the challenging clients.

Another aspect of self-awareness is knowing if you have hot buttons because then you can either warn people about them or prepare in advance how to handle them. For example, if you know that money is a huge stressor for you, then it's going to be extra critical that you and your partner put together a realistic budget at the beginning of the planning process and stick to it. Make sure that your total budget number is something that you are 100% comfortable with because if it's not, you're just going to stress the whole time about how much you're spending.

Empathy Matters

I would be remiss if I didn't touch on a person's ability to empathize as a component of emotional intelligence. Empathy refers to a person's ability to truly understand another person's experience. Empathy goes beyond saying "I'm sorry" to someone when they are going through something difficult and instead requires the capacity to get in the moment with that person, stand beside them, and experience what they are experiencing. In the simplest sense, empathy means that you are attuned to and actually feel what another person is feeling.

The ability to empathize will be necessary when planning a wedding if your partner is having a harder time with things emotionally than you are. Maybe your partner has some lingering hurt or trauma from past relationships and experiences bubbling up during the planning process. Or maybe your partner is struggling with divorced parents who are being more divisive in planning this wedding than they are coming together. Helping your partner in stressful situations will require that you empathize with them and really understand how they are feeling.

> **Here's an example of an empathetic response:** "I'm so sorry that you're feeling this way and that this process hasn't been enjoyable because of _____. Your emotions are totally understandable and valid. Please know that I am always here if you want to talk more about this. Let's figure out a game plan for wedding planning going forward so that we can try to make this a more pleasant experience for you."

The need to have empathy during the wedding planning process may be required with people other than your partner, too. You might have to empathize with one of those divorced parents when they express discomfort at seeing their ex at your wedding. You might have to empathize with a member of your wedding party going through a nasty breakup who just doesn't have the capacity to be what you need them to be right now. Having empathy will help you navigate and preserve those relationships while also keeping you from taking things too personally during an already emotional time.

Setting Expectations

When talking about wedding planning, it's important to recognize a long-standing societal belief that contributes to a lot of the emotional drama associated with weddings: The idea that your wedding day will be the best day of your life. *Way to put on the pressure, right?*

This thought that your wedding day will be so amazing and that it's going to define you leads to so much stress and anxiety when planning a wedding. How about we do ourselves a favor and push all of that aside?

I've got what might be some devastating (though hopefully liberating) news for you: **Your wedding day is NOT going to be the best day of your life.** Yes, it will hopefully be a pretty great day, but in the case that it's not, don't let that ruin you. If you don't believe me, then take the logical approach. If your wedding day is the best day of your life, then it follows that everything else is downhill after that. You're essentially peaking on your wedding day. That doesn't sound right, does it? There is so much in store for you after your wedding, whether it involves your career, maybe starting a family (whether it be with human or fur babies), traveling and having so many fun adventures, perhaps even jumping out of an airplane. If you approach your wedding day as the best day ever, then you're taking away space for any memorable event to come after. Make sense?

Instead of putting so much pressure on yourself to craft this incredible day and to feel a certain way in that moment, let's reframe how you think about your wedding. I always tell my couples that they should focus on their wedding as being one of the rare occasions in their lives when all their favorite people in the world will be gathered together in one room to celebrate. That's not going to happen a lot in your lifetime, so enjoy and be present for the magic that comes along with having your community surround you with love. You don't need to create a flawless, picture-perfect event where you feel that life won't get any better. Imagine how freeing it will be to view your wedding as this unique moment to immerse yourself in love and friendship and to eat, drink, and dance the night away.

And while we're at it, let's dispel the myth that your wedding must look a certain way and follow certain traditions. We've all seen what a wedding is "supposed to look like" in movies and on TV, read the stories about fairytale romances, and heard friends and family recount picture-perfect celebrations. There is, admittedly, so much pressure for a wedding to follow a specific playbook. But in case no one else has told you this yet, your wedding can be whatever you want it to be. You don't have to bow to society's standards for a wedding, your family's standards for a wedding, or even your friends' standards for a wedding. You. Do. You.

One of the most important things I do for my couples at the very beginning of the planning process is give them permission to do whatever they want for the wedding, and I make them a promise that I will help them make their wedding day reflect who they are as a couple. Love dogs? Great! Let's use miniature gold-painted dogs as your escort card holders. Obsessed with sweets? Wonderful! Let's create a dessert bar like no one has seen before. Have an inside joke about Sesame Street between you and your partner? Terrific! Let's get you Bert and Ernie cake toppers. Frankly, the sky is the limit when it comes to making your wedding unique and true to you and your partner. Let's agree to throw aside stale traditions and expectations if you want.

The wedding ceremony is a component of the wedding day rife with traditions that can stay or go. Whether it's who stands on which side (did you know that the tradition of brides standing on the left stems from being on the "proper" side in case the groom needs to draw his sword to protect her?), or the idea that there should only be one aisle, or who traditionally walks down the aisle and with whom (and that's all before you even get to the ceremony itself!), there is a lot to keep or discard. One of my clients was conflicted about who she would walk down the aisle with for her Jewish ceremony. Traditionally, she would be accompanied by both of her parents, and there would still be that component of "being given away" to her partner once she reached the chuppah. That idea didn't sit well with her, so we decided that her parents would walk down the aisle together during the processional and she would walk in on her own, meeting her partner at the chuppah with full agency over her decision to get married and not being "given" to anyone.

You'll notice many stories like this within these pages, and they all revolve around the same idea: making choices that feel right for you and your partner.

Been There, Done That

– by Shirin Eskandani

Founder of Whole Hearted Coaching

My husband and I had what you would call a whirlwind romance. We met, got engaged in 14 months, and got married two months later. It's definitely not what I had imagined when I first dreamed of getting engaged or married.

I had always thought my engagement would include a shower and lots of parties and that the wedding would be a big family affair. But, due to personal circumstances, my husband and I had to get married within two months. And honestly, what seemed to be a nightmare at first was the greatest thing that could have happened to me.

I am a Type A planner, and I knew that wedding planning for me would involve months of research, binders, and Pinterest boards. I would have spent hours going back and forth on details like the napkins and cutlery. I would have driven myself, my family, and my fiancée mad with all of my worries. But when I found out that we would only have two months to plan everything, I had to let go of what I *thought* was important and figure out what truly *was* important.

There wasn't enough time to overthink it all, so I had to let go of my controlling tendencies and trust that it would all fall into place. *And it did.*

The first thing my husband and I did was figure out what we wanted the day to feel like for us. The words that resonated with us the most were community, connection, joy, and play. Once we got clear on how we wanted to feel, we then figured out how to make it happen. We decided on a courthouse wedding with immediate family attending and a small reception afterward. We knew we wanted an intimate celebration with lots of yummy food and good music.

The first task on my list was finding a wedding dress. I had always thought finding my dress would be like a scene out of a TLC reality show. But instead, it was me scouring online for the perfect outfit and accessories. I was lucky that planning for the wedding happened during winter sales, and I was able to find TWO wedding outfits at a steep discount. They were both perfect and more amazing than I could have imagined. I bought them thinking I would return one, but I ended up wearing both (a 60s inspired tea-length dress to the courthouse and a 70s inspired white jumpsuit at the reception).

Overwhelmed by figuring out all the logistics, I sent out an SOS to our local friends, and they came through. One donated her gorgeous loft; another offered her catering services; another volunteered to be our photographer. *Each and every part of our reception was made possible by our community.*

I always say that our wedding was a "surprise" wedding because I had no idea what it was going to look like. I had left the decorations, food, and flowers up to friends, so when I arrived it felt like the most incredible surprise. I entered our reception and was greeted by tealights, candles, flowers, and so much love.

Our wedding was perfect. We were surrounded by some of our closest friends and family, ate amazing food, danced the night away, and celebrated my and my husband's love.

My favorite part of the night was the impromptu speeches given by our friends and family. None of it was planned. It was all from the heart. It felt so intimate because each and every person there knew us both on such a deep level.

That night taught me that a wedding is a celebration of your and your partner's love. The details like the napkin color and floral arrangements are wonderful, but they're not the most important thing. I realized that all that stuff is superfluous. What made that day so incredible was being able to truly celebrate with our community. To this day, our friends tell us that it was the most fun and memorable wedding they had ever been to.

We are now planning a bigger wedding so that all our family and friends can attend. This wedding is important to us because some of our dearest couldn't attend our small impromptu gathering. The most important intention for this wedding is family.

COVID-19 has put a wrench in a lot of our plans, and sometimes I'll find myself reverting to my old ways, trying to micromanage every detail. And then I remember what is most important. To us, what truly mattered was our love and our families.

I am so grateful for our small intimate surprise wedding; it taught me so much and allowed me to have the wedding that I never dreamed of... in all the best ways.

Chapter 2:
The Big, Uncomfortable Talks

These important discussions will frame your planning and marriage

What You'll Learn:

- Having early discussions about significant life changes can help get you both on the same page, in the same book, or just at the same library. *It's important!*

- Getting in sync with your partner means having important discussions early on. From taking each other's names to having children in the future, knowing you share a vision can make the wedding planning process even easier.

- Money talks—*literally*! Get ready to talk about dollars and cents when wedding planning and in your marriage.

- I fully believe that the most awkward conversations are the most important. You might be surprised at how these talks bring you closer together as a couple.

You know how people pre-wash their dishes before they put them in the dishwasher or how they'll clean before someone comes to clean their home? Well, in the case of a wedding, you kind of have to plan out some things before you actually start planning, and part of that pre-planning is going to involve some big, uncomfortable talks. As awkward and uncomfortable as some of these talks may be, they are absolutely necessary to ensure a smooth road ahead.

Name Changes

There seem to be BIG expectations in whether you or your partner will change your last name after you're married. There's obviously the tradition (and assumption) that a woman will take the last name of her husband once they are married. Logistics aside (I hear it can be a huge pain in the ass to change your name legally), there's also a matter of identity – how you identify to begin with and maintaining your sense of self and independence.

I personally did not take my husband's last name, and I made that decision for a few reasons. Firstly, I was 30 when we got married, which means I had an established career by that point and a distinct identity as Leah Weinberg. Secondly, I'm technically Jewish, and while I don't practice or consider myself at all religious, it was still important to me to maintain my culturally Jewish last name. Thirdly, I wasn't comfortable with the honorific "Mrs.," indicating that I "belonged" to my husband.

I say this is something to discuss in advance because one partner might have assumptions that the other partner is going to take their last name after the wedding, and when that doesn't happen, it might cause some serious conflict. Better to work that out early on and make sure that it's something that the two of you can overcome. A friend of mine got married but didn't take her husband's last name, and his reaction to her "feminist bullshit" (among many other things) is what eventually led to the two of them getting divorced.

Depending on how passionately you and your partner feel about these things, there are numerous options to consider:

- Both of you keeping your names
- One partner taking the other partner's last name (there are lots of men who have taken their wives' last names.)
- Hyphenating
- Moving your last name to a middle name and then taking the other's last name as your own
- Creating a whole new last name for both of you! (My husband and I have for years toyed with the idea of becoming the Brownbergs.)

I'm confident that you can reach a decision that's mutually agreeable and will save you from being caught off guard later on by the other person's feelings.

The Kids Talk

Another expectation-setting conversation and important topic for couples to get on the same page about before they say "I Do" is regarding children. Start with the obvious; do you see a child or children as part of your relationship together? Can you imagine yourself as a parent? Do you *want* to have a child and be a parent?

For most of my adult life, I've known that I have zero interest in being a parent to any kind of human. Fur babies on the other hand? I'm here for that. Because I know how important a topic like this can be for people, I brought it up very early in my relationship with my husband. And knowing me, I probably brought it up *inappropriately* early in our relationship. (I admit later on to having the worst timing when it comes to having important conversations.) Fortunately, my husband felt the same way as I did, and we could move forward in our relationship knowing we were on the same page about this. I also told my parents long before I got engaged that I would not be having kids because I felt like I needed to set their expectations too.

This talk goes deeper than just deciding whether you and your partner see children in your future together. You should talk about whether having biological children is important or whether adoption would be an option. You may have to talk about which partner will physically carry the child or whether you want to have a surrogate. Based on prior experiences or people's medical histories, you may have to talk about what paths you're open to pursuing to have a child. And you also must talk about timing because that's also something you and your partner need to agree on.

Division of Wedding Planning Labor

Ah, the age-old assumption that...

> (a) all weddings have a bride and a groom, and
>
> (b) the bride does all the wedding planning work.

Let's pretend those dated ideas don't exist anymore, shall we? Society tells us that wedding planning is a woman's job, but what if, for example, two women are getting married? Or there's not a woman getting married? Or one of the partners is non-binary? Or a man and a woman are getting married, but the woman has an incredibly demanding job while the man has a lot of free time on his hands? According to society, who plans the wedding then?

It's going to be incredibly helpful at the outset of the wedding planning process to determine how you and your partner will divide the wedding planning tasks. And you should definitely *not* default to any traditional roles. First, determine what each partner's strengths and weaknesses are. Maybe one partner is a whiz at internet research and compiling spreadsheets (great for collecting information on prospective venues and vendors!). Maybe the other partner has a solid creative mind, which is perfect for focusing on the aesthetics of the wedding and what elements make up that vision.

Next, consider your work schedules and whether one partner's free time exceeds that of the other. It's not fair to put the majority of the work on the shoulders of the person working until midnight every night (and on weekends) when the other partner is home by 6 p.m. and has their weekends free.

Another consideration is how excited each partner is to plan a wedding. One partner might be super busy at work and loathe internet research, yet they are pumped to plan a wedding. That's certainly a point to consider when dividing up wedding planning tasks. When my husband and I got engaged, I was working full-time as an attorney and hadn't yet dipped my toes into the wedding industry, but I was *so excited* to plan my wedding. Even though I had a ridiculously large workload and didn't have the most patience for online research, I knew that I wanted to take on most of the wedding planning tasks. But instead of just taking over the process, I had a conversation with my husband to make sure he'd be ok with that (he was) and to find out what tasks he wanted to handle himself. In the end, he took ownership of researching and booking our getaway car and the honeymoon. Because we had a conversation to establish our roles, I never once felt resentful for taking on the majority of the planning, and he never felt left out of the process.

So, know your strengths, know what time you have available, determine how much work one partner may *want* to take on, and then divide and conquer accordingly. Trust me; it's going to save you from a lot of complaining about your partner to anyone who will listen down the road.

Money

My therapist says the top three things that couples argue about are sex, children, and money. We'll leave the sex and children topics for another day (and another author), but let's talk about money when it comes to planning a wedding. My guess is that it's the number one stressor for couples during this time, just ahead of things like family dynamics and blending cultures or religions. So, get ready, folks; things are going to get a little uncomfortable because, if you're anything like most people, money is *not* your favorite topic.

With every prospective couple, I'm quick to dive into questions about their budget. Of course, I'll get to know a little bit about them first (when did you get engaged, how did you meet, what's your vision for your wedding), but before we get too far into the conversation, I always ask about budget. It's not meant to be icky or to seem like all I care about is money, but let's be honest; if a couple's budget and my fees don't line up financially, I don't want to waste either party's time.

Like it or not, money is at the core of wedding planning because, unfortunately, the details of your wedding depend on how much money there is to spend. So, what can we expect to confront during the wedding planning process when it comes to money, and how do we handle those situations?

Get Curious About Beliefs Around Money

Because money is such a loaded topic, you should do some self-reflection and have conversations to identify what money means to you, your partner, and any stakeholders (family or friends who will be financially or otherwise involved in wedding planning) before determining what the budget is for your wedding. (More on that later.) Here are some important questions to consider when you begin the planning process:

- Are you very conservative with money and don't like to spend?
- Does your partner spend money more freely?
- Does either of you tend to spend more than you have?
- If your parents are going to be funding the wedding, how do they view money?
- Are they happy to contribute their money to your wedding? Or will there be some resentment there because maybe they feel obligated to pay for your wedding but happen to be super uncomfortable spending money generally?

These hypothetical questions can go on and on. Still, the key here is to ask these questions before you dive into your wedding budget and to have thoughtful conversations whenever any friction arises.

The Financial Heart to Heart

At some point in your relationship (whether it's early on, or once you get serious and talk of marriage is on the table, or right after you get engaged),

Trae Bodge, a lifestyle journalist and TV commentator who specializes in smart shopping, recommends that you and your partner have what she calls a "financial heart to heart." She says it's imperative in a relationship to sit down with your partner and talk brass tacks about money. And it's better to do this sooner rather than later.

In this talk, you and your partner need to be honest about:

- How much each of you earns
- How much you both have in savings
- What investments each of you has
- How much debt the two of you carry (whether it's student loans, credit card debts, car loans, etc.)
- Anything else related to your finances

If you're ahead of the game and have this chat before you get engaged (hats off to you!), then there's an ancillary conversation to have once marriage is officially on the horizon. And that conversation involves how you and your partner will handle your money *after* getting married.

Consider discussing:

- Will you co-mingle all your money, or will you keep everything separate?
- Will you have one joint account that you each contribute to for household expenses while still maintaining separate accounts for personal expenses?
- If you go the joint account route, will each of you contribute to it equally, or will the contribution be proportionate based on each of your earnings?
- Aside from where the money comes from, who will be responsible for physically paying the bills?

I know; it's a lot to sort out. And it's going to be uncomfortable, but I urge you to push through the discomfort and awkwardness because, believe me, having this squared away nice and neat *before* getting married will save a lot of headaches later on. And if at any time during these conversations you and your partner hit a roadblock, ask for help from a financial planner. That person will know all the right questions to ask and will be able to guide you to a mutually agreeable result. If speaking with a financial planner doesn't feel like the right fit for you and your partner, Trae recommends finding another place of comfort (whether it's at your place of worship, with a therapist, or with family or friends) to have these conversations and break down the barriers around money.

Prenuptial Agreements

Frankly, prenuptial agreements get a bad rap. I can recall countless movies and TV shows that I saw as a kid where someone getting married felt conflicted about whether to ask their soon-to-be-spouse to sign a prenup or where a wedding was called off because one of the partners asked for one.

As I got older and could formulate my own opinions on such a controversial topic, I began to see both sides. Yes, I can understand how one partner asking the other to sign a prenup has an underlying insinuation that the other person is entering into the marriage in some part for access to money. But at the same time, if that's not your motivation, why are you getting so offended?

Talking with your partner about a prenup will likely be a weird, awkward, and potentially difficult conversation, but it is a critical component of open, honest communication with your partner. Prenups used to just be for wealthy people, but today they are much more common. I encourage you and your partner to have a conversation to determine whether it could be right for you. And if it is something you want to look into, note that you and your partner will need to retain separate attorneys to manage the process for you so that both sides are equally and professionally represented. It may also be something you want to allocate money for in the wedding budget.

I want to acknowledge that the following is just my personal opinion (though I hope it would receive support from the financial planners, divorce attorneys, and therapists reading this), but what I'm about to write is critically important, so please take a minute to let it sink in.

 **PRO TIP:** In many cases, people get divorced because they are not the same two people who entered into the marriage. *I'm going to say it again; people get divorced because they are not the same two people* who entered into the *marriage.*

Of course, at the time you're getting married, your partner would never dream of asking you, for example, for any of the money from your trust or for an ownership interest in your business because they plan to be financially stable themselves throughout your marriage. But if you find yourself in the unfortunate position of getting a divorce down the road, you two are no longer on the same page regarding your relationship. And odds are you are different people than you were at the beginning of your marriage. Why have to argue about anything at that point? Why not have a plan in place from the beginning that will dictate how things will go down if you part ways?

I've always been fascinated by couples who have been married for decades (over 20+ years) and end up getting divorced. In some cases, I observed a common thread of becoming empty nesters and staying together only until their kids are out of the house. But in many cases, the reasoning wasn't clear.

At one of my previous law firms, a divorce attorney rented office space there, so when we were on a project together, I asked him this burning question of mine about how couples who have been together for so long can decide to get divorced. His answer was simple: In many of these cases, the two partners have grown and changed, and they didn't grow or change together. They became different people who were no longer compatible with each other. That's obviously something neither partner could have foreseen when they said their "I do's" all those years ago.

You and your partner never know what's going to happen in the future. Obviously, the two of you hope you never even need the prenup, but why not put one in place now to save you the time, energy, and heartache down the road if circumstances change? Think of a prenup more like a planning tool rather than an accusation of one party's motives or intentions. The term "prenuptial agreement" is most definitely a term that comes with a lot of baggage, but why not change your mindset on it and think of it as a smart, responsible thing to do as part of your wedding planning process?

The Guest List

This one might seem out of place to you, but in my experience, couples have a very, very hard time agreeing on a guest list. Preparing an initial draft of your guest list is one of the very first logistical things you should do when you start planning a wedding for two reasons: one, the money factor, and two, the emotional factor. It's obvious to most couples that more people means more money for food and booze, but how your headcount impacts your budget in other ways may be less obvious. First and foremost, a big guest list means a venue appropriate for that size, so you may have to pay more for a venue to get more square footage to physically hold all of the people you want to invite.

More guests also mean more rentals. You must rent tables (plus linens) and chairs to seat each person, and then you're renting plates, glassware, and utensils for each place setting. And for each table you have, you'll likely have floral centerpieces or some other type of décor, so the money is adding up in that regard, too. One of the most common issues I see with inquiring couples is an estimated headcount that's not supported by their estimated budget, so at the outset of planning, you must get these two things in sync.

Aside from being able to afford your guest list, you've got to decide who is on it in the first place. Your guest list should be comprised of meaningful individuals who you love and adore and who you very much want to be present on your day. But realistically, I know there will be pressure to invite people who don't necessarily fit that description.

PRO TIP: Guests should have a thoughtful place in your day and should not be invited out of "duty." If you're feeling pressure to invite people you don't want out of obligation, you have the power to say no. For example, are you worried your boss is expecting an invite? Politely let them know you're having an intimate celebration with just family and close friends.

I obviously don't know the ins and outs of a couple's family dynamic when we first start working together. Still, I try to encourage them to be discerning when it comes to who they *want* to invite and who they *have* to invite at the direction of parents and other family members. Are your second cousins really a must-have for the guest list? Will a non-invite result in family members not speaking to one another? If you're on a limited budget, then inviting your parents' friends who you've barely interacted with over the years (or maybe never even met) isn't, in my opinion, the best use of two spots on the guest list. But if parents are funding the wedding, then maybe you have less of an ability to push back there.

I've found that couples who have parents or others contributing funds have a hard time saying "no." So, let's practice one way to have that hard discussion:

> "Hi [fill in the blank]. We wanted to speak with you about inviting [_____] to the wedding. While we know it would mean a lot to you to have them there (and it would be more fun for you to have them there), we're trying to be really thoughtful with our guest list. It's important that the people there on our wedding day are people we know and have relationships with. We'd be uncomfortable with having someone there who feels like a stranger. We hope you can understand why that's so important to us."

Aside from obligation invites, you may also find yourself feeling the need to invite someone out of guilt.

Guilt invites include:

- Your co-worker who has been your rock in the workplace but who you've only known a year
- Your best friend from high school who you haven't seen or spoken to in years
- Someone that invited you to their wedding but you aren't close to anymore
- Your childhood babysitter who you know it would mean a lot to them to attend, but they've stayed in touch more with your parents than with you

Crafting a guest list can be an emotional and difficult process, especially when you're trying to limit your numbers. It's a moment when you identify who your nearest and dearest are and then make that public knowledge. It's easier said than done! Even when you are being mindful of obligation and guilt invites, knowing who to keep and who to cut can still be challenging. The question I suggest my couples ask when they are having a tough time with their guest list is, "Would I be upset if I didn't get an invite to this person's wedding?" If the answer is yes, then it seems like you're close enough with them to warrant an invite. If the answer is no, well, then it seems you have your answer.

I know that this chapter has given you and your partner *a lot* to think about, and none of these discussions are going to be fun or particularly easy, but I hope you can understand that they *are* necessary. Creating that foundation for your marriage and your future is critical and talking about these things is a big part of that. I'm personally a big fan of getting everything out on the table and then working through it all step by step.

Been There, Done That

– by Justin McCallum

Owner of Justin McCallum Photography

When weddings are already so naturally tied with family, the planning process can bring up even more emotions for adoptees. Personally, I was dealt the added stress of reconnecting with members of my biological family (also known as birth family) in the midst of the planning process.

I was lucky to be adopted at less than two months old by a loving and supportive mother and father who have been my incredible family ever since. About 25 years later, I took one of those spit-in-a-tube genealogy tests to determine my heritage, but I later learned the service can connect relatives based on your DNA, too. I was unexpectedly contacted by a member of my biological family – a second cousin who couldn't figure out how my Irish surname fit into her distinctly Italian family tree. This sparked an interest for me to learn more about my biological family and search for information about my birth parents.

While this was a novel and exciting journey, the desire to know more about my biological parents felt tinged or like an unspoken taboo. I didn't want to slight my adoptive mother and father, who raised and provided for me, and I worried expressing interest in my biological family would make them feel as if they weren't enough.

Having to discuss this intrinsic but atypical aspect of my identity felt like coming out of the closet all over again, so I found myself putting it off. But not being forthright with my parents about trying to connect with my birth family felt like the omission of something shameful, which I didn't want to perpetuate either.

My parents were facing the brunt of the heavy lifting with our wedding, both financially and creatively. They were inviting the most guests, lived closest to the wedding venue, and had the most time and resources available to contribute to the planning and design. They were total rock stars, and we couldn't have done it without them, so the last thing I wanted to do was seem ungrateful by focusing on my "other" family. On top of not knowing how to talk to my adoptive parents about the discovery of my biological relatives, there was the question of how - if at all - to include my birth family in the wedding.

It was not an easy topic to broach amid a myriad of other stresses of wedding planning, but I should have known my parents would be thoughtful and supportive, just as they always had been. They easily understood that my desire to know more about my biological roots didn't lessen how much I cared about them, and they welcomed the situation as a part of our story. In the end, we opted not to include my new blood relatives in the invite list since I hadn't met any of them in person yet, but we eventually got to meet and gather as a modern, blended clan after the big day.

"I'm going to be blatantly honest with you for a minute: None of the information you are going to find online or on wedding blogs about the "average" cost of a wedding in your location is going to be accurate."

– Leah Weinberg

Chapter 3:
Making Financial Sense

It really is all about the Benjamins

What You'll Learn:

- It's going to take some effort to determine how much things actually cost and the best way to go about it.

- Remember that you aren't in a competition with anyone but yourself. Your wedding doesn't have to be the best on Pinterest or Instagram; it must be the best for *you*.

- The decision of whether to self-fund or accept outside contributions to pay for the wedding is a complicated one. I'll help you make the right choice for you and your partner.

- Financial woes in wedding planning happen when expectations don't match reality. Have conversations about finances and planning first, so money doesn't cause you strife.

How Much Does It All Cost?

Now that you've done the inner work, set expectations, and had some big talks, the next step in the wedding planning process is to understand what your wedding budget is going to be. To do that, you need data. And with regards to that data, I'm going to be blatantly honest with you for a minute: **None of the information you are going to find online or on wedding blogs about the "average" cost of a wedding in your location is going to be accurate.** Within a town or a city, there will be venue and vendor options at every price point imaginable. So, even within the same place, what a wedding costs is going to vary significantly. Sure, you can find info on what you can expect to spend, but will that amount match the wedding you've been envisioning is the real question.

Admittedly, getting a grasp on what things cost is a tricky part of the budgeting process. If you're working with a wedding planner, then based on your style and overall vision, they'll be able to give you a pretty accurate sense of what things are going to cost. If you don't have a wedding planner, my suggestion is to reach out to venues and vendors that catch your attention and ask them for pricing information. You can let them know that you're in the budgeting phase, you love their venue or their work, and in the interest of preparing an accurate budget, you'd like to get pricing information.

Need some help on exactly what to say to a venue or vendor?

> "Hi there,
>
> I'm recently engaged and absolutely love [your venue] [your work]! To make sure that I'm putting together an accurate budget for my wedding, it would be really helpful to get a sense of your pricing. Do you have some information that you could send over?
>
> Thanks in advance!"

 **PRO TIP:** If you're a couple whose inboxes are pretty full already, consider creating a wedding-specific email to use for the wedding planning process. That will help you keep your personal and work email separate from wedding planning emails, and you won't have to worry about being signed up for wedding-specific newsletters after the wedding is over.

Avoid the Pinterest Trap

Social media can be great for helping couples visualize what a wedding would look like at their venue or for coming up with clever ideas to infuse some personality into their day. But it can also be a terrible distraction when couples start to confuse what *they* want for something someone *else* wanted and when their budget can't accommodate all the grand ideas contained in the images they've been saving.

For example, I know some couples get really focused on specific poses or images that their photographer (or even another photographer) has captured, but it's not realistic to expect that you can replicate that exact image on your wedding day. Other couples have their hearts set on publication-worthy tablescapes with luscious flowers, candles galore, and custom linens that cost ten times more than what the couple had budgeted.

Comparison is a natural part of being a human, so know that comparing your wedding plans to something someone else has done is normal and to be expected. But it's one thing to be inspired by something another couple did and another to try to copy or outdo another couple. To make sure you're not crossing this line, take a look at your intentions and your feelings when you're looking at inspiration images. Is it making your creative juices flow, allowing you to develop some fun plans for your own soirée? Or is it making you feel jealous or bad about yourself because you can't compete? To keep yourself from falling into the comparison game, be sure to check yourself whenever you start feeling a certain way when you're looking at others' weddings. And as always, unfollow people on social media who don't make you feel positive about your own life—it's not a competition.

 **PRO TIP:** This is a particularly prevalent issue with inspiration images. There's a severe lack of information available on what things actually cost, so couples naturally get their hopes up for a certain look, only to realize that it's outside their budget. And don't get me started on the cost of wooden farm tables.

To Self-Fund or Not to Self-Fund, That Is the Question

Once you have a handle on approximately what your wedding budget will need to be, you must determine how the wedding will be funded. Here's one big question to answer: Are you paying for the wedding or allowing others to help? In answering that question, you'll need to take a look at your household finances and determine what you and your partner can contribute (or feel comfortable contributing). Do you have the ability to cover the wedding budget you've determined you need? If so, do you want to spend all of that money? One of my couples had a large amount of money in savings but knew that children would be imminent after the wedding and wanted to make sure they had the money for that, which played a role in determining whether they fully funded the wedding themselves or accepted outside contributions. (In case you're wondering, they ended up accepting outside contributions to preserve their savings account for future life events.)

When deciding whether to self-fund your wedding, if you've looked at your finances and don't think you can afford the wedding you've budgeted, you have to ask yourself whether you want to scale back to create a wedding you can afford by yourselves or whether you want to have others contribute so you can have the wedding you envision in your minds. If you want to self-fund but don't quite have all the funds you need for the wedding you want, one option is to have a longer engagement to give you more time to save. And if you go that route, you must have a specific plan for what you'll put in savings each month and be committed to sticking to that plan.

One of the biggest pros of self-funding your wedding is the autonomy that it gives you in planning the wedding and making decisions. But even with that independence, to maintain the relationships with those around you, you should consider how you can still make family and friends feel involved in the process. (Though the caveat to this is you should only do what feels comfortable for you.) For example, if you're not particularly close to a parent, keeping them in the loop on all wedding planning decisions might feel uncomfortable or disingenuous. But asking them to attend a tasting with your caterer or baker, having them join you to pick out your day-of attire, or getting them involved in the floral design process could be great ways to include them in a very distinct and limited role. Also, you can always ask the person what would make them feel like they are part of the planning process. Open and honest communication is my go-to in these situations.

If one of the biggest pros to self-funding your wedding is autonomy, then it stands to argue that accepting money from others to pay for the wedding sometimes means giving up control. If you decide to accept outside contributions, there is *a lot* you need to know. Read on for my thoughts on navigating that scenario.

If family or friends are going to give you money for the wedding, there are two important things to determine at the outset. The first is to find out how much money they are going to give. I fully realize that it is immensely uncomfortable to tell someone that you need an exact dollar amount for how much they will contribute, but you honestly can't plan a wedding without that information.

With one of my couples, one partner's parents had agreed to pay for the wedding but were not clear on what size that financial contribution would be. That made it incredibly challenging to start planning the wedding because planning for a $50,000 wedding would be different from a $100,000 wedding and even more distinct from a $200,000 wedding. I honestly didn't even know what venues to show this couple. In that case, I started by putting together a budget for them based on the cost of venues and vendors I generally worked at and with, and then the couple took that budget to the partner's parents for approval. You've got to keep in mind that you can't plan a wedding in a vacuum, so, unfortunately, you need to know how much money you're working with.

The second determination that must be made when someone other than the couple is contributing financially to the wedding is what role in the wedding planning process that money is affording this person. And again, you've got to ask pointed questions to get to the bottom of this. Ask the person contributing what their expectations are as far as the money is concerned. If parents are paying for the entire wedding, do they expect to be consulted on all financial decisions, or are they happy taking a back seat and simply writing checks? In other words, what strings are attached? It sounds a little cold to approach things this way, but you've got to understand what comes along with that money for you and your partner to make the informed decision of whether to accept that money with the conditions attached to it.

If at any point during the planning process it feels like someone wants a level of control that you and your partner are uncomfortable with in exchange for their financial contribution, have a conversation about whether their contribution is worth what comes along with it. You may also have to examine whether not accepting that money or not having that person involved in the planning process will negatively impact your relationship with that person. At that point, you're asking what relationships you need to hold onto and which ones you can let go of. If the relationship is not worth losing, sometimes you have to compromise to save the relationship.

When these conversations aren't had at the start, it can lead to a lot of conflict down the road. One of my couples had a family friend contribute money to pay for a handful of elements for the wedding, including live music for the ceremony and flowers. When it came to selecting the musicians, the family friend had no interest in weighing in and totally trusted the couple's choice of who to hire. With the florist, the couple had gotten a proposal from a florist they absolutely loved, but the family friend insisted that they get a second quote from a florist she knew. The couple obliged but still really preferred the florist they had found initially.

They shared this opinion with the family friend, and much arguing ensued *for days*. Several days into the arguing, the couple let me know about what was going on. On the one hand, they loved the first florist and felt terrible that she had been holding the date for them. On the other hand, the family friend was very important to them and was responsible for the bill. After a lot of internal consideration, the couple concluded that they couldn't risk the relationship with the family friend by overriding her on this decision. Setting expectations at the outset can go a long way in helping to avoid a clash like this.

Unless you have someone paying for the entire wedding, a really helpful approach to setting expectations is to assign an element of the wedding to coincide with someone's contribution. For example, if Uncle Scott is a musician and he's giving you $15,000 for the wedding, you can let him know that you'll be using his money to hire the band of your dreams. And you should also ask him whether he wants to be part of the process of selecting a band with you. Keep in mind that if he does want to be involved, and you know he has far different musical tastes than you, you may want to think twice about accepting his offer.

 **PRO TIP:** As a practical matter, when others are paying for all or part of the wedding, I suggest that you have them transfer that money to you and your partner so that the two of you can handle payments with your vendors directly and be the ones signing all the contracts. Your vendors will appreciate the straightforward approach, and it just makes the administrative side of things a lot cleaner.

In addition to creating an environment susceptible to conflict, a sometimes unexpected feeling that can arise when someone else is paying for the wedding is…. *guilt.* You or your partner may feel guilty in general for accepting such a large amount of money from someone. You might feel guilty that your parents are spending all of this money on the two of you, *or* you might feel guilty that your partner's family has more to contribute than your family. I helped one of my couples navigate the latter scenario.

The bride was Indian, and the groom was not, but they had decided to have a more traditional Indian wedding with events like a Mehndi party and sangeet in the days before the wedding and traditions like a baraat the day of. They also had a desired guest list of 200 people. Budget conversations with this couple ran the gamut from whether they should self-fund the wedding (which they had the funds to do, albeit on a more modest scale), to whether they should let the bride's parents pay for everything (which her parents were more than happy to do), to whether we could create a budget that would allow both sets of parents to contribute equally with the couple funding whatever else was needed (which would have resulted in the groom's family paying the maximum amount his family could afford and the bride's family paying far less than her family could afford).

Because of what the couple wanted for the wedding and what all of the parents wanted for the wedding, it quickly became clear that this wedding would require a rather large budget. The only way to meet the budget was to have the bride's family pay for the wedding.

My first step in helping this couple was to present the different budget options and show them what a wedding would look like at different price points so we could ultimately determine who would fund the wedding. After that decision was made, I then had to get the groom comfortable with accepting the financial assistance from his soon-to-be in-laws. My emotional appeal centered around the fact that the bride's parents would not be giving them this money if they weren't over-the-moon excited to do so. They love their daughter, they love him, and they want to support this marriage. That's really what that money meant. And then my logical advice to him was that you literally couldn't have the wedding that everyone wants without accepting that money, so you need to decide what wedding is going to happen here.

After our chat, and I'm sure after some more internal discussions, both the bride and groom got comfortable with having the bride's parents pay for the wedding and having the groom's parents pay for a welcome dinner the night before for about half of the wedding guests. I'm sure this couple didn't go into the planning process thinking they'd hit this wall so early on, but through open and honest conversations (as well as some critical thinking), they came to a solution that made everyone happy.

If there ends up being a disparity between what each family can or will contribute and the family contributing less feels like they will be less involved as a result, think about ways to make sure they feel included in the planning process. Have them attend certain appointments or maybe give them tasks, like helping to pick out save the date or invitation designs online. And depending on how crafty they are, bring them in on creating some décor or small elements for the wedding day.

Discussion questions to help you determine whether to self-fund or accept outside contributions:

Based on the research you've done for the wedding you want, can the two of you afford to pay for the wedding yourselves?

o If yes, determine whether you want to spend that money on the wedding or continue to save it.

▪ If you prefer to save it, move to the other main question below to make sure you're comfortable asking for and accepting help.

o If no:

▪ Then ask: Can we opt for a longer engagement to give us a chance to save up for what we need?

▪ Move to the other main question below to make sure you're comfortable asking for and accepting help.

Are there outside contributors who have volunteered or who you could ask (and are comfortable asking) to help pay for all or part of the wedding?

o If yes, you need to ask them (1) how much they can contribute and (2) what level of involvement they are expecting in connection with their contribution.

• Based on how they respond to the first question, and if the amount they can contribute won't pay for the entire wedding, you will need to determine whether you want to pay the difference yourselves or modify your vision for the wedding to fit what they can contribute.

• Based on how they respond to the second question, you need to decide if you can accept the conditions attached to their contribution or if you would rather decline their offer.

• If you decide to decline outside contributions, then you can either pay for the wedding you want yourselves (if you have the means to do so, whether currently or by saving up), or you can modify your vision for the wedding to fit what you can financially afford today.

Actual Spending

Now that you've now determined how much your wedding is going to cost and how much money you have to spend on the wedding, it's worth noting that you don't have to spend all of the money that's available to you. In some cases, the budget might be big enough for a 200-person gathering, but the thought of having that many people causes you anxiety, so you and your partner opt for something more intimate that happens to cost less money. In other cases, as I've experienced with some clients, they simply don't *want* to spend all of the money that's available to them. Doing that can give them comfort that there's padding if something amazing pops up that they do want to invest in, or that they (or outside contributors) aren't spending so much on the wedding, or that there's money they can put in the bank for an amazing honeymoon or towards a down payment on a house.

I also want to add a note here about pursuing financing to pay for your wedding. I personally do not support the idea of going into debt for your wedding because I don't think it's necessary or the best way to start a marriage. When asked about this topic, I always say that if a couple can't afford the wedding of their dreams today, they should have the wedding they *can* afford. Then, three, five, ten years down the road, when they've got more money to spend, they should throw a kick-ass anniversary party (maybe with a vow renewal!) that will function as the party that they originally wanted.

Money is already an uncomfortable topic for most people. Having to have direct conversations with others about giving you money, how much they can give, and what expectations come with those funds makes it far worse. I get it. But I'm sorry to say that these conversations must be had, and I recommend having them early; otherwise, you'll likely encounter a good bit of conflict and might even be putting some relationships in jeopardy.

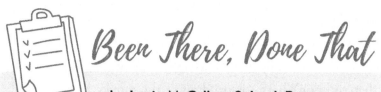

Been There, Done That

– by Justin McCallum & Jacob Passy

Justin - Owner of Justin McCallum Photography
Jacob - Personal finance reporter

Going into wedding planning, we anticipated some of the external pressures we would face as a queer couple from people who didn't accept our love. What we didn't expect was that budgeting and the financial aspect of the wedding would be one of our greatest challenges.

The tradition most people grow up with is that the bride's parents are the ones to pay the bill. Obviously, neither of us was a "bride," so we initially tried to approach things in as egalitarian a manner as possible, with each of us and our respective families taking on roughly the same costs associated with the big day.

But as the guest list was formed, we quickly realized that wouldn't work. Our wedding was held just outside Justin's hometown, and he has a rather large family – he has over a dozen cousins alone, not counting their spouses. Meanwhile, Jacob only had five relatives in attendance, including his parents and sibling. Had things been kept equal, Jacob and his family would have been financially responsible for almost five times as many guests as they had there.

Plus, our two families had differing views on how much a wedding should cost, with one preferring a more lavish celebration and the other erring on the less expensive side. And since Justin is an only child, his parents didn't have to think about saving for future nuptials, while Jacob's parents had to save for his younger sibling's potential future wedding costs so they could match the contribution.

All of this was a recipe for tension during the planning process. Nothing came to blows, thankfully, and eventually, we all came to realize that keeping things egalitarian didn't mean equal contributions by splitting the bill 50-50.

Ultimately, with queer weddings, there is no "rule book" or set expectations to follow. It's a double-edged sword: We felt free to create the wedding we truly wanted, but we found that making the rules up as you go can be more stressful than you might realize.

"My advice on how to stick to your wedding budget is pretty simple. Point blank, JUST STICK TO IT."

– **Leah Weinberg**

Chapter 4:
Working with Your Budget

Spending with your brain, not your heart

What You'll Learn:

- You might find yourself asking for discounts from prospective vendors. The reason why might surprise you.

- The myth of the "wedding markup" is just that, a myth.

- Consider your budget your North Star when it comes to spending money. Revisit it every time you're about to spend money as a gut check.

- What savings can a planner offer you in the wedding planning process? Hint, it's probably not the savings you think.

Asking for Discounts

At this point, you have your wedding budget, and now you're ready to start booking your vendors. When my couples get to this stage, I can often anticipate the following question: Should we ask for a discount?

I'm not going to lie; this is a complicated question. On the one hand, I know vendors who get offended when couples ask them for a discount. They (rightfully) feel somewhat disrespected and that the couple doesn't value the service that the vendor is offering. In justifying this reaction, they'll say something like, "You wouldn't ever go into your dentist's office and ask for a discount, would you?" *They're not wrong.*

On the flip side, I totally understand *why* a couple is asking for a discount (because, frankly, I was guilty of this, too, when I got married!). Requests for discounts often arise out of a combination of fear and wanting a "win." Let's break down exactly what I mean here:

- There's fear in not knowing what you *should* be paying for something. Most couples have never gotten married before, and if they (a) aren't working with a planner, (b) don't know anyone who works in the wedding industry, or (c) don't have friends that have gotten married recently and in the same area, they have no barometer for what a wedding costs. They are perpetually afraid of overpaying for something or being ripped off. And that's understandably terrifying. *However, you can't let fear guide your financial decisions, right?*

- There's fear in spending large sums of money. Chances are the wedding is the first time a couple has ever spent money of this magnitude. A normal human reaction to spending large sums of money is hesitation, worry, nervousness, stress, and… well, fear!

- Getting a discount feels good. For some people, it might be a pride thing – you feel superior because you negotiated a lower price. For others, receiving a discount might justify your fear that you were overpaying to begin with. At the simplest level, getting a discount is a win, and getting a win undeniably feels good.

This is where doing your due diligence can come in to help you feel less afraid. Research what venues and vendors cost in your area. Preferred vendor lists from venues can also be a helpful place to start since that's generally a list of trusted professionals whose pricing is complementary to whatever the venue charges. Ask around. Find out if your friends have friends who have gotten married recently or ask around at work. Join Facebook groups for engaged folks. I've seen how helpful those groups can for people getting married, well beyond getting a grasp on how much you can expect to spend on a wedding where you live.

Knowledge is power. Once you're armed with facts and numbers, you're going to feel much more confident when it comes to spending money on your wedding and be able to stop acting out of fear.

The Myth of the "Wedding Markup"

Ah, the mythical wedding markup. Yes, you heard me. It's a myth. And not because it doesn't happen, but because charging more for a service for a wedding than for any other type of event is justified.

Please believe me when I say that the higher price companies charge for weddings is based on the additional work they will put in because it's a wedding and not another type of event. For example, a makeup artist is hired to do makeup for a person for their 40th birthday party. I imagine the email exchange is brief: the makeup artist and client confirm a date and pricing, the client probably sends over some inspiration photos, and there may or may not be a trial at some point.

With someone who is getting married, the email traffic and pre-wedding calls and meetings will probably be triple that of any other event. There will be a trial. Maybe multiple trials if the person isn't happy or is indecisive or changes their mind. There will be an intense day-of schedule to coordinate makeup services for ten people (the person getting married, members of the wedding party, family, etc.) in conjunction with the hair schedule. There will be last-minute changes to said schedule as people opt out of having their makeup done. There will be emotions leading up to the wedding day and on the day itself that the makeup artist will have to navigate that wouldn't normally be present when doing makeup on someone for another occasion.

Comparing the planning of a book launch party to a wedding might be a helpful visual here:

	Book Launch	Wedding
Planning Time	Three months from the booking date to the event date	18 months from the booking date to the event date
Event Duration	Two hours plus an hour on each side for set up and breakdown	Six hours from guest arrival to the end of the reception, plus four hours for set up and an hour for breakdown
Stakeholders	Just the author	The couple plus three sets of parents (one partner's parents were divorced)
People to Coordinate on the Day-Of	Just the author and the vendors	The couple, immediate family, and a 14-person wedding party (plus the vendors)
Photography	Two hours of coverage of the event only	10 hours of coverage for getting-ready photos, portraits, and the wedding itself from start to finish
Catering	No tasting. The author ordered drop-off catering from a menu.	Multiple tastings to determine the dinner menu
Florals	A $500 budget for bud vases for cocktail tables	A $12,000 budget to transform the entire venue
Music	A Spotify playlist from an iPhone	A 12-member live band
Hair and Makeup	For just the author	For the bride, the bride's mom, the groom's mom, the groom's stepmom, and seven bridesmaids
Hotel Blocks	Not needed	At three hotels
Transportation	Not needed	Coordination of shuttle pick-ups from three hotels

There is unquestionably a higher amount of work involved in providing a service for a wedding, and a vendor MUST charge for that increased work. At this point, you might be thinking, "Well, that might be true for some vendors but not all vendors. What about a limo driver? There's no way they could be doing more work if it's a wedding versus any other kind of event." *Oh, but there is.*

 **PRO TIP:** Transportation is probably one of the trickiest vendors to coordinate for a wedding and is the most prone to delays (simply because of the unknowns of traffic, guests being late getting on the shuttle, etc.). As a result, I spend a lot of time with transportation companies creating detailed and realistic schedules. You better believe I confirm those schedules multiple times and always make sure to get driver contact information (which means I'm bugging these companies up to the day before the wedding). Transportation for other events is far less complicated and can be much lower stakes, so it makes sense that the cost of a limo would be more for a wedding than another type of event.

If you receive a quote from a vendor who you love, but it's a bit out of your budget, a way of asking for a discount is by inquiring whether you can streamline the vendor's services (put a limit on email communication, limit the number of calls or meetings you can have, set a start date for when email communication can begin) to lower the cost. This allows the vendor to decrease their amount of work for a lower price rather than asking them to provide the same amount of service for less money. That being said, not all vendor categories can streamline their services and still provide quality service on the wedding day, but you can absolutely have the conversation to see what's possible and to set expectations.

Sticking to Your Wedding Budget
If you've followed the advice I've given you on preparing a budget thoughtfully, then my advice on how to stick to your wedding budget is pretty simple. Point blank, JUST STICK TO IT.

That budget is the product of level-headed, informed decisions. It was created at the beginning of the planning process when you carefully determined what you were comfortable spending and how you wanted to spend the money. There was a lot less emotion involved than when you find yourself in the middle of planning wanting an epic floral installation at your venue that is well outside what you wanted to spend. I have many couples who get to the end of their planning process and are so wrapped up in the excitement and joy of the day approaching that they start spending emotionally.

As I see it, there are two types of budgets in a wedding: the stated budget and an emotional budget. While a gigantic ice sculpture at cocktail hour detailing the place you met is, no doubt, a nod to how you want to tell your story, it's also a great way to spend thousands of dollars in one fell swoop. When you're looking to add elements to your big day that aren't in line with your stated budget, ask the following questions:

- Why do I want this addition?
- Is it a must-have or a nice-to-have?
- What will this addition bring to the day?
- Is this a consideration because I have some "found" money to spend? If so, is there a better investment I can make with that money for the wedding or, alternatively, should I put that money in savings?
- Is this addition something guests will experience for the entire wedding, or does it have a limited role? (E.g., the ice sculpture mentioned above that's only at cocktail hour.)

Always go back to that stated budget. It will help you avoid frantic money spending. And you'll thank me later.

Can a Wedding Planner Actually Save You Money?

This is one of my favorite questions because I get to toot my own horn a little bit AND hopefully encourage you to hire an essential professional for your vendor team. The short answer to whether a wedding planner can save you money? *Totally.* The long answer? Yes, but not in the ways you might be thinking. Let's break down the ways a planner can save you money, piece by piece.

Emotional Savings

Finding your venue, booking your vendors, creating your day-of timeline and floor plan, coordinating logistics with all of your vendors - a planner is there to take care of these obvious details. But your wedding planner is also going to be able to do so much more. We are there to give you a sense of confidence during your wedding planning process that you're making smart decisions and that nothing is going to slip through the cracks. We're also on-site to ensure that everything will be 100% taken care of on your wedding day.

I want my clients to feel calmer and less stressed when planning their weddings. After so many weddings, I know that everything they're going through is normal, and my goal is to make them feel less alone, even during the times that they swear they're the only people who have ever gone through this same experience before. If couples face tricky family dynamics and feel lost, I help them navigate the emotional elements and focus on the bigger picture – their marriage! If they feel completely overwhelmed and paralyzed by all of the options available to them, I help them break the decisions down into smaller pieces to be more manageable. The saved time and energy of these situations are invaluable—so my couples say.

> "We couldn't have had as smooth and relaxed of a wedding day as we had if it weren't for Leah's help. She takes such a burden off of your shoulders throughout the whole planning process. You never have to worry about whether you are behind schedule or if there is some detail you are not thinking of because she is on top of all of it. She

has a really wonderful way of listening to her clients and letting their preferences and vision come through, while also giving her expert advice when you need it. We never felt like she pushed us in one direction or another, but when we were stuck on something, it was so helpful to have her there. We started working with Leah in the summer of 2019 for a September 2020 wedding, and we certainly didn't have any idea that COVID would upend our plans. Leah was so compassionate as we figured out how to revise our wedding plan to be pandemic-safe. We struggled with whether to postpone or cancel, and she helped us think through the pros and cons, gave us a sense of what other clients were doing, and really helped to guide us through the decision. She was able to be sympathetic and give us the space we needed while also encouraging us to make decisions as the time grew closer. We ended up canceling our big wedding and had a small backyard ceremony. We then had to essentially re-plan our wedding to fit that new plan, and Leah was totally calm and on top of it! Having her on our team was a true comfort and such a huge help throughout our whole process. Our wedding day felt truly relaxed and so happy - we knew we didn't have to worry about any details or logistics because Leah would be on top of it!" – Rebecca & Mike

In addition, I'm helping my clients to hire vendors that are trusted professionals and who are a good fit for them personality- and style-wise. If they are interested in vendors I haven't worked with before, I can vet those vendors and make sure that they will do a good job on my clients' wedding day. Hiring someone who gets my thumbs up gives my clients a ton of confidence in their decision-making. Because of that, there's going to be a lot less second-guessing of their decisions and buyer's remorse.

I recently had a couple looking to hire a videographer for their wedding, which can be tricky because there are many stigmas around videographers. I hear from a lot of my couples that they don't want the typical "cheesy" wedding video (though everyone's definition of "cheesy" seems to be different). Then there's the misconception that videographers are going to be obtrusive and have a camera in your face the whole day. I'm here to tell you that a good videographer isn't going to do either of these things. But back to my couple....

Once they were ready to start looking into videographers, I sent them a handful of options that I felt were a good fit for their style and their budget. They had a preliminary call with one of my recommendations but weren't sold. They came back with a videographer they had found online and asked if I could reach out to that company. Since I wasn't familiar with the company, I asked around in my planner network to see if anyone had any experience with them. Multiple people told me that working with this company had been a hot mess, from the unprofessional behavior of the videographers who showed up on the wedding day to the deliverables being unacceptable to a client and needing to be sent back for a complete re-edit. Without my couple having me there to look out for them and their best interests, they could have gotten themselves into a real pickle by hiring that company.

Spending Smarter

A good wedding planner is worth their weight in vendor relationships, and I pride myself on my roster of vendors. I will look at the aesthetics and budget of a client's wedding and introduce them to vendors at various price points so they can splurge where they want to and save in other areas. My experience with different venues comes with knowledge of hidden costs at each venue. I will ensure that my couples select a venue that will help them stay within their budget because that seemingly affordable loft space might take a client over their budget once you factor in renting kitchen equipment, obtaining permits, bringing in all the furniture, and other necessities to host a wedding there.

I like to be transparent about things, so I act as a gut check for my clients if something feels too expensive or unnecessary. Any good wedding planner will help you spend your money efficiently so that every dollar counts.

I touched on asking for discounts above, and it's worth noting that what a wedding planner can do for you when it comes to venue and vendor discounts will vary from planner to planner. I personally like to be very upfront and candid about discounts – in general, I do not feel comfortable promising them. While I have been able to negotiate discounts with some vendors in the past, I don't want a couple to book me on the premise that I'll save money because if that doesn't happen, I don't want them to be disappointed or feel like I misled them in any way. Let me put it this way: book your wedding planner for their expertise, relationships, and knowledge, not their discount ability.

While there are no money-saving guarantees in hiring a wedding planner, a good wedding planner is there to stretch your dollars further than you could yourself, help you identify potential money pitfalls, and put you in touch with incredible wedding professionals, no matter your budget.

Been There, Done That

– by Trae Bodge

Lifestyle journalist and TV commentator
who specializes in smart shopping

My husband and I got married in 2004, so it's been a while, but if I remember correctly, our budget was like, "as little as possible." I'm kind of joking, but at the time, we didn't have much money, so we were very price-conscious. While we didn't always agree on the details, thankfully, we were on the same page with spending.

Money was tight, so we didn't want to take on extra debt, but we also acknowledged that our wedding was a once-in-a-lifetime thing. We were prepared to scrimp, save, and DIY, but we didn't want the wedding to feel like that. I think what saved us was that we were not interested in what "the Joneses" were doing. Comparing yourself to others can be a real trap for some people. We didn't feel like we had to impress anyone.

In spending our money, we got creative with everything. We spent a fair bit on the venue because we wanted to have the wedding over a weekend with our closest friends and family members. We chose a bed & breakfast with a lot of bedrooms so everyone could stay. But then guests paid for their rooms, which were less expensive than staying at a hotel, and that contributed to the overall fee. Food was also important to us, and we wanted to feed everyone for the weekend, so we spent a bit on that. My maid of honor and others contributed to the cooking outside of the wedding meal, which was catered. It was a delicious yet very casual-style meal with paper plates – which I'm sure a snooty person or two frowned upon – but we didn't care, and it saved us a lot.

When it came to paying for the wedding, our parents contributed some money, and we self-funded the rest. Our parents didn't have a lot of money either, so we checked with them first to see what they could do and then looked at what we could manage outside of that.

For what our parents did contribute, we loosely assigned certain expenditures to people, but it was understood that we would handle everything and would have the final say on what we wanted. We wouldn't have accepted money under other circumstances.

I remember that my husband's family paid for the liquor. They gave us a sense of what they could afford, and we worked within that budget. We wanted an open bar, so we limited the booze to beer and wine, which is much less expensive than a full bar or even a signature cocktail. We were also very fortunate to have a friend who worked in the wine industry who worked out a generous discount on the wine.

And then there were friends and family who contributed their skills – way better than a wedding gift! Our graphic designer friend designed our invitations, my maid of honor helped create the bouquets, and my dad's girlfriend altered my wedding gown that I bought at a non-profit that donated proceeds to women in need. Overall, it was a very collaborative effort, which I think lent a certain flavor to the whole event.

In terms of whether we stuck to our budget, I think we did! It helped a lot that we asked people to contribute to our honeymoon in lieu of gifts, so we didn't have to worry about needing money for our trip. This was before there were websites and apps for that sort of thing, so my maid of honor collected all the contributions (and I returned the favor for her a couple of years later!). We never looked at what people gave. All we knew was that we had just enough to take a three-week trip to Thailand, Laos, and Cambodia. We scrimped on some things (a couple of hotels) and splurged on others (a 5-day scuba diving excursion), and it worked out just right.

With regard to post-wedding finances, we shared a couple of credit cards but kept our bank accounts separate for a few years after the wedding. It was working out fine as is – we had even purchased an apartment together! But it was always in the back of my mind that we should combine finances at some point, so after we sold our apartment and bought a house, we set up a joint account. But even to this day, 16 years in, we each keep our own bank accounts and only move funds into the joint account for bills.

My advice for those getting married: don't allow finances to diminish your joy. Figure out what works best for the two of you and don't be afraid to do things differently than others.

"The moment we figure out, 'What are we honoring?' [is key]. Sometimes someone's like, 'It's not even the details of my culture, but it's about honoring my family and what my family feels like,' or '[It's about honoring] where I come from,' and that can give us so many answers for how something needs to look then."

– Meera Mohan-Graham

Chapter 5:
Crafting a Wedding that Feels Like the Two of You

Keep your big day personal and incorporate your values and culture

What You'll Learn:

- Ask what you need to honor, and then work with a team to make your vision a reality.

- Infusing traditions into your wedding day is a reminder of what's to come. Giving grace, compromising, and allowing your partner to feel heard will solidify your relationship and help you both grow.

- Blending cultures and religions into a ceremony and wedding day can pose a challenge. Ensure everyone (including your family) feels heard by asking what's important and utilizing a third party if you need an outside opinion.

Wedding planning isn't always linear, and sometimes you'll be focusing on multiple things at the same time, so somewhere amidst determining your wedding budget (because the reflections you make in this chapter may impact how much money you have to spend to make it happen), you're going to start having conversations with your partner about what a wedding that represents the two of you actually looks like. I'm not talking about what your menus look like or what songs you're going to have your DJ play. I'm talking about identifying what makes you *you* and what makes your partner *them,* and how the heart of each of you is going to be represented that day. If you're a couple blending different religions, cultures, or backgrounds, or if you or your partner are a member of the LGBTQ+ community, then these conversations could be even more in-depth.

In creating this chapter, I've brought in an expert in the wedding world who has more professional experience with this subject than me and who has a more appropriate life experience to speak on this topic than me. Please meet Meera Mohan-Graham. Meera is a wedding planning advocate and coach who works directly with couples to keep them connected throughout the planning process, help them navigate the emotional and interpersonal aspects of planning, and support them in translating shared values into specific planning decisions. Meera's ability to guide couples through these topics merges her work as a personal coach with her former work as a documentary wedding photographer. Though she no longer documents weddings, she still incorporates photography into her work with her couples through an intimate couple's session that she facilitates and documents in person as part of celebrating who they are.

Says Meera, "I'm queer. My husband is trans. I'm a woman of color, of South Indian descent. I'm the daughter of immigrants. I come from a lineage of interpersonal trauma. I kind of come with all of these demographic considerations, and the result is that the people that started coming to me [as clients], also were coming from complex backgrounds or were people of color or marginalized."

I mentioned earlier how, at the start of our relationship, I give my clients permission to have the wedding they want and that feels like them. Meera takes that idea to a much deeper level. In working with her couples, one of the first things Meera does is give her clients a sheet that says, "You have permission to ____." And the first permission that she gives is, "You have permission to care about your wedding." Whether it's permission to care about your wedding while in a global pandemic, or permission to care about your wedding when someone close to you is sick, or permission to care about your wedding despite many wedding traditions being rooted in patriarchy and capitalism, she lets her clients know that it's ok, and starting from that place of permission can be very powerful.

When it comes to working with couples who are blending religions, cultures, or backgrounds, she has noticed a trend amongst those couples where they dive immediately into the details. They start thinking about specific traditions or rituals that need to be incorporated and how those things will fit into the day before they've even addressed the bigger picture. In those situations, Meera encourages her couples to take a step back and answer questions like:

- What do you need to honor about your culture?
- What do you want to feel?
- How do you want to feel about the experience of seeing two cultures honored?
- How do those tie back to honoring yourselves and your relationship or your communities or families?

Through this exercise, couples may come to realize that part of what's driving their thoughts and actions is a pressure to be the sole representative of their culture or a feeling that their family is the sole representative. And if that's the case, Meera reminds them to get out of the weeds and take a high-level approach to work through it. "The moment we figure out, 'What are we honoring?' [is key]," says Meera. "Sometimes someone's like, 'It's not even the details of my culture, but it's about honoring my family and what my family feels like,' or '[It's about honoring] where I come from,' and that can give us so many answers for how something needs to look then."

Once couples get clarity on what they are honoring and how they want to feel, they can also dive deeper into what each component of the wedding means to them. Meera, who likes to instill in her clients that every part of the day should have a purpose and a meaning, doesn't want people to mindlessly incorporate elements into their celebration because they feel like they must. She and I talked about the tradition of walking in for the ceremony and how what that means to each person will be completely different.

Is it a moment to walk through your community and feel the love and joy coming from them? Is it a moment to walk towards the future with the person you love? Is it a moment to walk with someone down the aisle and honor their place in your life? Is it a moment to walk together with your partner and have that be a declaration of your partnership? That moment can mean so many different things, so it's important to determine what it signifies for you. Explains Meera, "An entire process can become poetry when you start taking it away from what it used to be or why it was done a certain way. And you say, 'Well, what does it mean? Why do *I* make the choice?'"

To the point of the importance of having a wedding that feels like you and your partner and giving yourself permission to have the wedding you want, Meera adds: "It's worth mentioning that people need to remember that queer weddings are not straight weddings and that [the people getting married] have the right to honor their queerness. Depending on the people and what personal work they've done, there's this [idea that] 'These family members have never seen a queer wedding and we need to prove that it's just like a straight wedding because their acceptance means so much that they're doing this for us,' right? So, there's this tension between that and the right to honor the fact that you are a queer couple. And if that needs to be honored, manifested, said in some way, you deserve to do that."

As you uncover these deeper meanings for your wedding and everything involved, it will hopefully be a little easier to envision how your wedding will be representative of both you and your partner.

Bringing Family into the Conversation

When Rana and Sarah hired me to help plan their wedding, one of the first details they mentioned was that Rana was Indian, Sarah was Jewish, and neither of them was particularly religious. One of their goals for the wedding was to incorporate elements of both religions and cultures into their wedding ceremony so that both families would feel represented and included.

We moved forward with that plan, and they booked a beautiful venue for their Fall wedding. A few months into the planning process, I get a call from Sarah – she says they've hit a major snag about ceremony planning. Because white is the color of mourning in India, Rana's family was opposed to Sarah wearing a white wedding gown during any portion of a ceremony that had Indian elements to it. Rana and Sarah, who had not anticipated that reaction given Rana's lack of connection to the Hindu religion, weren't sure how to handle the issue. Let the brainstorming begin!

We talked about incorporating an outfit change into the ceremony so that Sarah could wear a sari for some of the ceremony and then a more traditional white gown for the rest of the ceremony. But then we decided that it could be a little awkward to have guests sitting around while Sarah changed outfits. We talked about Sarah wearing a sari for the entire ceremony that would incorporate both Hindu and Jewish elements, but then Sarah's family didn't love the idea of that. We talked about making the Indian celebration an occasion all on its own – separate date, separate location, separate guest list – but then Sarah and Rana weren't too keen on planning two entirely separate and different celebrations.

Ultimately, we landed on doing two different ceremonies on the planned wedding date and at the same venue. The day started with a small breakfast for guests in the morning, immediately followed by the Hindu ceremony. After the ceremony, guests went back to wherever they were staying for lunch and an outfit change, while the couple, wedding party, and family took portraits in their Indian attire. Next, Rana and Sarah went back to their respective hotel rooms for their own outfit changes, and Sarah had her second set of hair and makeup services for the day. Before the Jewish ceremony in the evening, the couple, family, and wedding party gathered for more portraits, this time in their second outfits for the day. The Jewish ceremony was followed by a non-denominational reception with Indian cuisine, ensuring that all their guests felt comfortable and welcome.

This all made for an incredibly long day for the couple. Still, it was important to Sarah and Rana that both of their families were happy with how their cultures were represented and that both families felt like a welcoming environment had been created for their guests. Of course, they wanted to have a wedding that felt true to the two of them, but they realized at the end of the day that honoring their families' wishes was also a priority.

At the same time that you're talking about money with each other and family and figuring out how you want to represent the two of you at your wedding, you'll also have to have those talks with family if you're representing or blending cultures, religions, and backgrounds. My advice is to have those conversations with your families sooner rather than later. Make sure you understand your and your partner's expectations when it comes to incorporating religious or cultural traditions into your wedding day and also what your families' deal breakers might be (like no white wedding dress for an Indian ceremony). You may receive input that you weren't expecting or that you don't particularly want to hear, but it is by far better to have that information at the outset than to get so far down the road with planning that everything gets derailed when this information comes to light later.

And don't assume you know what your parents' wishes are going to be either. Plenty of couples have been surprised by a parent's insistence on religious elements in a wedding when that parent doesn't even actively practice that religion.

Another couple of mine was planning their Jewish wedding, and we were talking through the flow of their reception and what Jewish traditions would be incorporated. There was the hora, of course, but they also wanted to have a HaMotzi, a Jewish tradition of beginning a meal with a blessing over bread and then sharing the bread. Technically, a traditional HaMotzi should occur before anyone begins eating, so when you're planning a wedding, small details like whether the salad will be served before the blessing (because what if people start eating before the blessing?) are things you must consider. As we were planning the flow of the reception, I asked the couple if it would be ok for salads to be served while guests were dancing, and then a relative would give the HaMotzi once guests are seated. They said that was totally fine. But from past experience, I knew to have them ask their families if it mattered. It turns out my instinct was correct, and one of the parents did care that people might eat before the HaMotzi, so we held salad service until after the blessing.

What happens when parents or family are more passionate than the couple about having the wedding look a certain way or incorporating different religious or cultural elements into the day? Meera tells her clients that, in those situations, they have three responses to choose from: "Yes," "No," and "Compromise." And they will always have all three options to choose from. They can say "yes" to a request. They can say "no" to a request. Or they can agree to compromise so that both parties can have some of what they want.

Meera uses the example of a Hindu family that really wants the couple getting married to have a traditional Hindu wedding, but the couple isn't particularly religious and never imagined having a traditional Hindu wedding. "The discussion we have to have then is, 'How much does it matter to you what you do?'" explains Meera. "Because the answer's either going to be, 'It actually matters a lot, and those are not the traditions that we want to have.' Or, 'We want our choices to be a little bit different or modified from the standard traditions.' And sometimes, people are surprised to realize that the answer is, 'We actually don't care. We want this to be a joyous community day. So, we might be ok with a more traditional experience.'"

Couples often think that there's a rule that they must be deeply passionate about all of the choices for their wedding ceremony. But what if, instead, you realized that you were passionate about making your family happy and didn't care so much about exactly what you needed to do to make that happen. Continues Meera, "[It's] being able to [say], 'Actually, my family will be really happy, and my community would really celebrate with us. I bet the two of us would have a lot of fun doing that.' It doesn't have to be that deep. [It's] having the freedom to say, 'Actually it would mean a lot to me to give that to my family.'"

If you're having discussions with parents or family and seem to be making no progress, Meera suggests inviting them in: "Pick a thing that they can help with and invite them in. Because sometimes that just gives a person something to do, a way to share, a way to care." And if inviting them in doesn't work, then you've got to establish your boundaries with this person or these people. If you know that you're not going to get on the same page with them concerning your wedding, and their negativity impacts you, maybe you make it a rule that you just don't discuss the wedding. I know that may sound extreme, but wedding planning is stressful enough, and you've got to set boundaries to protect your mental, emotional, and physical health during this time.

Another option is to let family plan that part of the day if they feel strongly about the wedding being more traditional by their culture's standards. Petronella Lugemwa, an NYC-based wedding photographer who frequently works with multicultural, interracial, and interfaith couples, saw this with one of her couples. One partner was Vietnamese and the other was American. They wanted a very boho-chic wedding, but one partner's parents very much wanted to have Vietnamese wedding traditions included. Ultimately, they compromised and let the parents plan a traditional Vietnamese tea ceremony as part of the day, while the couple handled the remainder of the wedding and did it their way.

Says Petronella, "The couples who successfully navigate this have very clear conversations with the parents about, 'This is who we are, this is what we want, and this is what we're going to do to honor you.' They can then take parts of the wedding and say, 'This is what you have. This is your playground.' And that has been very, very successful."

The moral of the story? ALWAYS ask families for their input early on in the planning process unless you want to be unpleasantly surprised down the road, and remember that you will always have the option to decide how you'll respond.

Been There, Done That

– by Pooja Kothari

Owner of Boundless Awareness

I never dreamed of my wedding in that stereotypical way. When I thought about getting married, my mind always skipped to the reception, where I pictured myself decked out in a beautiful lehnga, dancing the night away with my friends. I could never picture who was beside me. Even after coming out to my family, I still couldn't picture who was standing next to me. I couldn't picture how a wedding could even happen. I had never seen a Hindu wedding with two women. After I declared to my world my sexuality, my fantasies of dancing in my beautiful lehnga seemed out of place. No one, it felt to me, celebrates two women getting married in a Hindu ceremony. The idea seemed so foolish to my deeply internalized homophobia. I didn't understand how to have the Indian wedding of my dreams with another woman.

But luckily, other brave people were more creative than I was. I saw my childhood friend get married to his husband in a Hindu ceremony. I saw a HuffPost article about a mixed-race, queer couple having their Indian wedding. People celebrated them. Our community celebrated them. My mind started to open about the possibilities very slowly, and marriage seemed possible. A year after dating Natalie, I told my parents I wanted to marry her. They said they supported me 100% and would be happy to pay for our wedding, whatever it looked like.

A week after my proposal to Natalie, she also asked me to marry her. We started talking about what kind of wedding we wanted, from no wedding at all to the courthouse to a simple ceremony to a full-blown two-day Indian affair. My wife is

Black, and I'm Indian. She grew up Christian, and I grew up Hindu. We talked a lot about what elements from our cultures we wanted represented in our wedding, how we could represent it authentically, and how much certain customs meant to us. Through our conversations, I kept coming back to an Indian wedding, and with Natalie's support, I finally accepted how much an Indian wedding meant to me and how badly I wanted it for us, for our friends, for our community of related and chosen family. But Hindu customs are completely dependent on gender, the gender binary, and a heterosexual couple. It took a lot of creativity from both of us to decide how to break all of that and make a meaningful ceremony that reflected our faiths and our lives.

"So which one of you is getting married?" was the question we got when we started looking at venues. I never wanted that question again or any other intrusive questions. I wanted this process to be as fun as it is for cishet couples. So, we started to pre-empt that question by calling ahead to wedding shops, ring stores and holding interviews with wedding planners, venues, and vendors. The first thing we always asked is, "Is your store LGBTQ friendly?" or "Hi, we are looking for a wedding planner; we are two women getting married in an Indian ceremony. How many queer weddings have you planned?" After that, every vendor we spoke to answered honestly and was gracious and respectful. The rest of the process was as fun (and stressful) as it is for cishet couples planning an Indian wedding!

One vendor that we struggled to choose was a Hindu priest. Who would officiate our queer Indian wedding and be willing to change pronouns, to change slokas that did not apply to our relationship dynamic, and to work with two women and deviate from the ancient wedding script? One of my best friends got married a few months before we did, and we found out the person who officiated their Indian wedding was not a Hindu priest but a family friend. I finally figured out who could officiate our wedding! Someone who knew both Natalie and me very well, someone who respected us deeply, and respected our agency and our wish to have a traditional Indian wedding that represented both of us: My mom!

Natalie and I celebrated our dream Indian wedding weekend in Brooklyn, New York, on October 14 and 15, 2016. The first night was the Sangeet - the pre-wedding singing and dancing night, which was held at Clovers Art Gallery on Atlantic Avenue. It included an amazing Bollywood dance medley from the dance team at SALGA – the South Asian Lesbian and Gay Association. Our wedding and reception were held at 501 Union Street, Brooklyn, New York. We had a beautiful orange and red mandap, a baraat with a dhol (a double-sided Indian drum) player to kick off the wedding, and my mom officiated the ceremony in Sanskrit and Hindi while my dad translated it into English for our guests.

Natalie found a gorgeous, embroidered gold and white wedding dress by the Indian designer, Payal Singhal, that she had shipped from India. My wedding shopping was with my parents in Edison, NJ. While shopping for lehngas and saris for the Sangeet, wedding, and reception (three different outfits, of course!), I did not mention my Indian wedding was a queer one except when it came to buying the mangalsutra. The mangalsutra is a wedding necklace that the in-laws buy for the bride. My mom passed down to me her mangalsutra, and my parents were buying Natalie's mangalsutra. Because the jewelry store employee saw me looking at the necklaces, she assumed I was the sister of the groom, shopping alongside my parents. She asked me, "So this is for your sister?" and I said proudly,

"No, I'm shopping for my future wife." She smiled at me in return. And then said quietly, "If I ever told my parents, they would never accept me." That's the thing about being queer in any community: around every corner, there is a constant fight for acceptance.

In the end, what made our interracial, interfaith, queer wedding the most memorable weekend of our lives, was our community: our related families and our chosen families. They made the Sangeet so entertaining, full of art, dance, and laughter. They made our wedding ceremony particular to us. They danced the night away at our reception and sent Natalie and me off with their blessings and support for our future.

A company's and business owner's core values may also come into play when you're selecting your vendors. If you are Black, Indigenous, a person of color, or a member of the LGBTQ+ community, it will likely be important to you that your vendor be inclusive, have a diverse portfolio, and create a safe space for your working relationship. If they are talking the talk, you need to make sure they are also walking the walk.

– Leah Weinberg

Chapter 6:
Hiring Your Vendor Team

Finding the right people for the perfect day

What You'll Learn:

- Identifying your priorities and understanding your decision-making style will go a long way in making the vendor selection process easier for you and your partner.

- Your vendors want to make your day spectacular. It's important to communicate openly about what you truly want and your expectations.

- Rule #32 in Wedding Planning: We don't hire family or friends.

What Are Your Priorities?

Congrats! You've survived an emotional onslaught just to determine how much money you must spend on your wedding and how to incorporate your and your partner's backgrounds to create a cohesive, true-to-you celebration. I applaud you for getting to this point! *But the work doesn't end here.* Now you're faced with how to break down that overall spending amount into categories for each of your vendors, and then you've got to go about actually hiring those vendors.

I touched on this previously, but it's an important point that bears repeating: Anyone who asks me about wedding budgets can expect to hear my rant about the lack of accurate information online about how much vendors cost and what a couple can expect to spend on their wedding in a given area. It drives me absolutely bananas. It's on my mind a lot, and sadly, I've yet to come up with a helpful solution. I'm starting to think maybe that's because there really isn't a solution. Stay with me here. It's not that I'm a pessimist; it's that I'm realistic about how much the cost of wedding vendors can vary, even in the same city.

Obviously, the average cost of a wedding in Los Angeles will be vastly different from the average in, say, Tulsa, Oklahoma. But even within L.A., couples can have a wedding for $15,000, or $50,000, or $200,000, or over $1,000,000. So, when budgets vary that much within a single city, how on earth is a newly engaged couple supposed to know how much things cost, and how is a website going to accurately tell you what an "average" budget is in Austin, Texas? Short answer? They aren't, and it can't.

The bad news is that couples are just going to have to do the research to find out what they can expect to pay for each vendor at their budget level. Start by asking friends who have gotten married where you live and who spent an amount on their wedding comparable to what you plan to spend. Reach out to different vendors just to see what they cost. Ask the question on social media – a great resource for getting information like this these days. Shameless plug: Hire a wedding planner who knows how much vendors cost in your area and save your own time and energy.

This research may seem annoying, but it's crucial for setting expectations. Going into the wedding planning process, knowing what you can and can't afford will be incredibly empowering. Having unrealistic expectations that ultimately get shattered is heartbreaking. Knowing *how* you and your partner want to spend your wedding funds is key to creating a realistic budget.

Now that you've got a general grasp of vendors (who you can afford with your budget) cost, it's important to determine your priorities when it comes to your vendors. Are you and your partner foodies, so having an amazing caterer outweighs spending a ton on florals? Are you both cool with saving money by hiring a DJ rather than a band? Is photography so important that you want to splurge on that superstar photographer and save everywhere else?

A good exercise is for each of you to separately write down your top three priorities when it comes to elements of the wedding and then discuss them together. If your priorities align, great! *Easy peasy.* If they don't, then you've got to dig a little deeper to understand why each of your priorities is so important. You have to be prepared to give things up and perhaps barter – "I'll give up X priority, but I need to get Y." This will hopefully allow you to create a compromise with which both of you can be happy.

Decision Making

Most of my couples feel pretty overwhelmed by the number of venue and vendor choices available to them, so, when working with me, I curate a nice, streamlined list for them of venues and vendors who fit their style and budget and who I also know and trust. But then I started working with Bron, and Bron needed *lots* of options. When it came to picking a venue, he needed to see every option available to him. When it came to picking a photographer, after reviewing my initial curated list of selections and his own handful of photographers that he'd found on Instagram, he asked to see my *entire* list of photographers I loved. Mind you, that list has 40+ photographers on it. I have no doubt that Bron pored over that list and researched everyone on it.

On the flip side, Dan and Jeremy preferred no more than three options per vendor category, systematically reviewing each vendor's proposal, having a chat with them, and then swiftly deciding who they wanted to move forward with. It just goes to show that everyone makes decisions in their own way.

At the start of the wedding planning process with my couples, I always ask about their decision-making style. When it comes to the number of options they want to see, are they the type of couple who wants a finely curated list of three to four vendors to consider, or do they need to see the entire landscape of what's available to feel like they've made the right decision? Are they quick decision-makers, or do they like to take a little bit of time before making a decision? Are they the type that makes a decision and sticks to it, never looking back, or do they make a decision and then agonize over whether they made the right choice, always second-guessing themselves?

If you're not working with a planner who can help facilitate this conversation, it's helpful for you and your partner to have a chat at the start of wedding planning to understand what type of decision-makers you are. That answer will help inform how you move through the planning process and what systems you can implement to help set you up for success. For example, if you know that you and your partner hem and haw when it comes to making a decision, give yourself a firm deadline by which to make the decision and communicate that deadline to the vendor (like, "we'll get back to you by _____ with our decision"), so that you have some external accountability.

Also, it's helpful for couples to mentally prepare themselves to be absolutely overwhelmed by the number of choices they will encounter at the outset of the planning process when selecting a venue and their vendors, especially if they live in a big city. Analysis paralysis is a real thing, and couples will likely find themselves faced with so many options that they don't even know how to start the process of making a decision.

There's also the possibility of being under so much pressure to set a date and pick a venue or vendor that the couple moves too fast. Maybe the couple moved too quickly in booking their venue and later decide that it's not the right fit for them. In that case, it's natural for the couple to feel a little embarrassed about not thinking the decision through well enough and also losing money in the process. When you hit that kind of stumbling block at the start of your wedding planning process, it can really put a damper on everything to come after that.

Sometimes you book a vendor who seemed great at the start, and then the relationship crumbled. If you find yourself in that position, assuming you can financially afford it, I always believe that the best decision is to part ways and then hire someone you're going to feel confident about having as part of your vendor team. If you do your engagement session and feel like you didn't click with your photographer, address that now rather than feeling uncomfortable having that person by your side for 8+ hours on your wedding day.

What to Look for in Your Vendors

We talked earlier about determining how you want to feel on your wedding day, and focusing on feelings is also going to inform your vendor choices. Think about sitting down to review photographer portfolios. When you've never hired a professional photographer before, it may be hard to differentiate between different photographers or develop the right words to describe what you like and don't like. So why not focus on how the photos make you feel? Can you feel the joy and energy of the day in the photos? Or maybe you resonate with photos that feel more intimate and focused on small moments. Or maybe you gravitate towards photographers who make the couple look like they belong in a magazine.

There's also the way that vendors make you feel when you interact with them. I always tell my couples (and frankly anyone who is engaged and asks for my advice) that, when hiring vendors, your first order of business is to make sure (a) they are a legitimate professional (What does their website look like? Are they on social media? Do they have good reviews?), and (b) that you can afford to hire them. When I recommend vendors to my couples, those first two boxes are automatically checked (one of the perks of working with a planner), so I have my couples go into meetings with prospective vendors with the purpose of getting to know that person and getting a feel for their personality. I also thoughtfully give my couples recommendations for vendors who I believe will be a good match style-wise rather than providing the same list of recommended vendors to all of my clients.

For example, I have a handful of DJs who are my go-to recommendations. If a couple is really knowledgeable about music and they are diehard music lovers, I have the best DJ for them. If a couple is really laid back about their music choices and just wants a great party, I know which DJ to connect them with. If a couple doesn't have strong opinions about music but likes to take a very organized, professional approach to their wedding planning, I have the perfect DJ to recommend. All three are different individuals. I'm good at understanding my couples' personalities and my vendors' strengths, so I often know what venue or vendor my couple will select before they even make a final decision.

Other questions to ask when considering vendors are: Do you feel a connection? Do you feel like they "get" you and your partner? Do you get a calming sense from the hair and makeup team so that you can be confident that they'll help keep the getting ready portion of your day super chill? Do you like your photographer's personality and look forward to having them be by your side for your entire wedding day? Did you click with a DJ or band leader personality-wise and get a sense that they really understand your vibe and musical choices?

I tend to say that if you're getting into a pros and cons list of vendors within a particular vendor category, then you haven't found the right person or company. I had a follow-up call with one of my couples after they had done video chats with prospective DJs. There was no clear frontrunner, and they started listing out the pluses and minuses of each person. I stopped them and said, "Let me go back to the drawing board and find you some new options because clearly, none of these folks are the right fit for you. I want to make sure you're working with a DJ that you love!" Your gut is going to tell you who the right vendor is for you (after the prerequisite reputable business qualifications, of course), so lean into what it's saying.

Particularly when it comes to hiring a photographer, you also want to make sure that you see yourself in a company's portfolio. If you are Black, Indigenous, or a person of color, you want to make sure that your photographer knows how to photograph and then edit your skin tone. Suppose you are a member of the LGBTQ+ community. In that case, it's important that your photographer has worked with other LGBTQ+ couples and understands that it's not going to be the same experience as photographing a straight couple. I heard about a photographer who asked in a Facebook group of other photographers something to the effect of "When you have two brides, how do you know which one to pose as the man?" If you're a member of the LGBTQ+ community, inexperienced people have no business being a part of your wedding.

A company's and business owner's core values may also come into play when you're selecting your vendors. If you are Black, Indigenous, a person of color, or a member of the LGBTQ+ community, it will likely be important to you that your vendor be inclusive, have a diverse portfolio, and create a safe space for your working relationship. If they are talking the talk, you need to make sure they are also walking the walk. A vendor's values should be pretty evident in how they interact with you and others, who they have worked with before, the words on their website and social media (are they still using "bride" and "groom" everywhere?), and the photos they share publicly. If they're not, it is 100% acceptable (and encouraged) to ask direct, pointed questions to determine how inclusive a potential vendor really is.

Even if you, as the person getting married, are cisgender, heterosexual, and white, hiring socially conscious and value-driven vendors may also be important for you. And even if it's not, keep in mind that it may be important for your guests. You don't want to make the mistake of including vendors in your wedding who might make your BIPOC or LGBTQ+ guests uncomfortable. A poorly-behaved vendor (whether they are making a racist comment or not honoring someone's pronouns) who will make any of your guests feel uncomfortable, unsafe, or unwelcome is something you want to make sure to avoid. So be conscious of that when considering who to hire for your wedding.

A Note on Family Members as Vendors

I have a strict rule regarding working with family and friends and their weddings: I don't do it. *No exceptions.* I would advise you to stay away from having any friends or family as vendors at your wedding. There are so many reasons for this rule, but for me, the biggest one is communication. It is very tough to have clear, direct, open, and honest communication with someone who you have a pre-existing personal relationship with. When one of your third-party vendors drops the ball on something, you'll have no problem pointing it out to them and asking them to make it right. If it was a family member or friend who let you down, you might hesitate to say something to them. On the flip side, when one of my couples is not making the best decision on something, I have no problem telling them. But if my couple were close friends of mine, I would think twice about how I communicated the same point to them.

Another significant reason has to do with preserving the relationship. Working with someone in a professional capacity can completely change the dynamic of the relationship or bring the relationship to an end. If you're working with a friend or family member as a vendor for your wedding and something goes seriously wrong, will you be able to forgive and forget? Will *they* be able to forgive themselves?

One of my client's parents owned a rental company in a neighboring state from where the wedding was taking place and, for a while, was contemplating providing the rentals for the wedding to save some money. I'll be honest; I was totally against the idea for multiple reasons.

First, the risk of something going wrong was just too high. The rental trucks would be coming from out of state and would likely have to arrive a day early and then park, fully loaded, overnight. My legal brain immediately goes into the litany of things that could go wrong. What if there was a weather event that prevented the trucks from getting into the city? What if the trucks were broken into while parked overnight? What if something was missing – with the warehouse located so far away, there would be no way to get a missing item. If any of this happened, if there were *no* rentals on the wedding day, how would the couple get out of this pickle? And would the parent ever forgive themselves for this misstep on their child's wedding day? In the end, both your wedding and your relationships are too important to risk anything going awry.

I recently had a prospective client contact me at the recommendation of one of my existing couples. I responded to the person's initial inquiry right away but didn't get a response for several weeks. When she finally responded, she let me know that there was some family drama going on (no surprise there!) that she was hoping to get sorted out before hopping on the phone with me. It turns out that one of her relatives, who is a wedding planner, offered to plan her wedding for free "as a wedding gift." Then the relative backed out, which is what prompted her to reach out to me initially. And then the relative came back in the picture, so she ultimately didn't need my services. We still ended up chatting, though, and she asked my opinion about having a family member as her wedding planner. I was candid with her and told her about my rule to not work with friends or family, and I explained why. She totally got it. In fact, her experience supported my reasoning because her relative had been completely unresponsive to her e-mails at one point. She knew that she couldn't e-mail her relative to tell them to get their act together and be responsive because there was a family relationship involved. Had she hired a third-party planner, you better believe she would have sent that planner an e-mail putting her on notice that she was unhappy with their level of responsiveness.

See? Hiring family hinders open, honest, and direct communication. And as I've said before (and will say many times again within these pages), communication is key to a smooth wedding planning experience.

Been There, Done That

– by Elizabeth Rosado

Corporate attorney and baking blogger

Planning a wedding is great practice for a successful marriage because it requires lots of communication, communication, communication. Adam and I had the good fortune of attending a LOT of weddings in the year or two before our own, and we took notes at each one. What did we want to emulate? What did we want to avoid? This helped us hone in on our priorities:

• We wanted the wedding to reflect who we were as a couple with as little interference by family as possible.
• We wanted a short and sweet ceremony without a lot of the usual stuffiness (no "love is patient, love is kind" reading for us).
• We wanted a fun party, but one where my very conservative and religious parents wouldn't feel out of place.

Having clear priorities simplified decision-making a lot.

Once we had our priorities, we had regular check-ins to make sure we were on track with planning and make sure we were sticking to our vision.

Because one of our priorities was to have as much control over the wedding as possible, the first decision we made was to pay for the wedding ourselves. Yes, it meant we had to be budget-conscious, and we recognize that not every couple has this option, but this decision meant we never felt beholden to the person signing the checks.

Of course, we still took our families into consideration and compromised on things that were important to them; it just meant that we could do it on our terms. For example, I was adamant that I didn't want to be "given away" or even walked down the aisle by my father (because FEMINISM). But I was surprised when my mom's one request was to walk me down the aisle with my dad. I initially resisted but eventually settled on a compromise that honored my parents without sacrificing my values. I walked part of the aisle by myself and then walked the rest of the way with both my parents (and no one "gave me away"). We also wanted Adam's father, a minister, to officiate, but we talked to him about revising his usual ceremony to better suit our values and our desire for a short ceremony. He initially sent us an outline that was nearly 20 pages long, which we stripped down to just a couple of pages. It was so meaningful to have my father-in-law officiate, and he completely respected our wishes to remove all references to "obey," lol.

When it came to choosing our venue and our vendors, we had to navigate a few things. First, my parents are very conservative and religious, so I knew they wouldn't feel comfortable with a raucous reception where there would be a lot of dancing and drinking. Many of our friends also had kids at that point, and we wanted a kid-friendly wedding. So, we chose a venue that would allow us to party with our friends but give folks alternative activities if partying wasn't their cup of tea. Our venue, the Museum of the Moving Image, was perfect! The exhibits remained open during our reception, and there was a cool video game exhibit at the time. All of our guests received tokens to play the games. So, my parents or folks with kids could duck away from the party and still have plenty to entertain themselves with.

I also wanted our catering to reflect my Puerto Rican culture, so we chose a vendor that could make rice, beans, and tostones, as well as prime rib and salmon. It wasn't "fancy," but it was perfect.

For our photographer, of course, we wanted beautiful photos, but it was also important to hire someone who would make our families feel comfortable and who could photograph people with varying skin tones. Not only are our families very diverse (I'm Latinx, and my husband is Black), but so was our wedding party. We wanted to capture everyone's beauty, so we hired a photographer who was a POC himself and had experience shooting large blended families.

Adam and I also wanted to incorporate a lot of non-traditional elements, so we needed a wedding planner who would embrace our quirkiness. We really lucked out with Leah; she really "got" us as a couple and didn't make us feel weird when we went outside the box with our wedding. She was enthusiastic when we decided to show movie clips instead of doing traditional readings and embraced our love of Star Wars (we had Han and Leia cake toppers, among other nerdy details).

While we didn't experience any overt acts of racism, we still struggled to find wedding inspiration that reflected the diversity of our family and friends. Most of the wedding inspiration I looked at during wedding planning was, well, white. This was most stark (and most heartbreaking) when I was looking for flower girl dresses for our nieces. It was nearly impossible to find Black or brown flower girls; I found maybe three or four photos that fit the bill, which I eagerly added to my Pinterest board. I've become accustomed to viewing whitewashed images, but knowing that my nieces couldn't see themselves reflected in these photos was really upsetting. We did end up finding great dresses for them, and they looked adorable and beautiful - I'm glad we could make them feel special on that day.

We did, however, experience a few instances of overt sexism. People would look to Adam when it came to financial points (even though I'm the primary breadwinner and contributed most of our wedding budget). And they would often leave Adam out of other decisions – instead turning to me – assuming he didn't have an opinion on color schemes or the order of the ceremony. We always wanted our wedding to be OUR special day but had to be very intentional about making decisions together because the wedding industry is very geared towards "brides," which is obviously antiquated (in more ways than one).

In the end, because we had clear priorities about what mattered, our wedding was perfect (for us).

"People are not mind readers. If you don't talk about what's bothering you, how will they know what's wrong?"

– **Leah Weinberg**

Chapter 7:
Your Communication Toolkit

Best practices for open and honest communication

What You'll Learn:
- Why communication is integral to navigating and thriving during the wedding planning process

- How to be an active listener and make sure that the people you speak with are *and feel* heard

Whenever my couples are faced with conflict during the wedding planning process, whether it's between each other or with family or friends, the first thing I recommend that they do to alleviate the conflict is to *talk about it*. After all, people are *not* mind readers. If you don't talk about what's bothering you, how will they know what's wrong? And let's not play the game of, "Well, they should know what's bothering me. I shouldn't have to spell it out for them" (which I am admittedly guilty of myself from time to time) because that only makes things worse. Not only does the other person still not understand what's going on, but now you're mad two times over - once from the original issue and *again* because you feel let down that they don't already know what's wrong.

Have you noticed that a member of your wedding party is acting distant? Talk about it. Are you frustrated that your parents are driving some of the decisions about the wedding? Talk about it. Do you feel like your partner isn't taking as active a role as you'd like in planning? Talk about it. Is your planner not listening to your wants and needs? The solution is pretty simple: Talk about it.

Specific Communication Skills to Master

To become a better communicator, you and your partner should focus on three specific skills:

• **Asking Questions:** Asking questions in a conversation can serve a lot of different functions. First, it's a great way to simply start a conversation, like asking someone how their day is going. If it's a tough conversation that you need to have with someone, asking questions can be a way to ease into the discussion in a thoughtful, proactive way. Asking questions is also helpful in gathering information in a conversation. Think of it as a research or fact-finding tool. You can use it to understand how someone feels about a particular issue or find out their ideas for tackling a joint task. Asking questions is also a way to convey to someone that you care about them and are interested in what they have to say. (Though to make that meaningful, you have to follow that up with active listening so that the person feels [and is actually being] heard.)

■ **Try It Out:** Create a list of questions to ask your partner about the wedding planning process. What is most important to them? Do they have a tradition they'd like to include? Is there anything that makes them nervous and anxious about planning a wedding? Knowing what your spouse-to-be wants, needs, and might be concerned about can help make future conversations easier.

• **Explaining:** Explaining is how you give information to the person with whom you are talking and how you can clarify the point or message you are trying to convey. Just saying something doesn't make it true, right? For someone to receive, understand, and believe what you are saying, providing an explanation and evidence of your commentary is necessary. In the context of a wedding, maybe you find yourself having to explain to your parents why you don't want them to invite their neighbors to your wedding. In that case, your explanation could address the fact that you've never met their neighbors, you don't have a personal connection to them, and that it's important to you that only those nearest and dearest to you are at the wedding so that it feels special and meaningful. If applicable, you could also include an explanation of the additional cost of inviting the neighbors. Whatever explanation you find yourself giving, make sure that it's clear and focused to up the chances that it's received and understood.

- **Try It Out:** When conveying a data-driven message, make sure you have the facts handy. What type of evidence will the person find most compelling? Are they someone who likes to see numbers? Are they most swayed when the message comes from a third-party source? How much data will they need to understand your point? Having the right type and amount of evidence to explain your position will help the conversation be that much more productive.

• **Listening:** Strong communication skills go both ways. Just because you've got a solid grasp on how to engage others by asking questions and conveying your own feelings with clear and focused explanations doesn't mean communication ends there. Being an active listener can go a long way. Here are some tips on how to achieve the perfect balance between communicating your feelings and listening to the feelings of others:

o **Focus:** Tune out or remove any distractions that will prevent you from paying attention to the other person.

o **Don't interrupt:** Let the person speak so that you can hear everything they have to say, and then you can respond. Interrupting doesn't help you get your point across; it weakens your position!

o **Ask questions:** If you don't fully understand what the other person is saying or getting at, ask questions to clarify. This will also show them that you're engaged and genuinely interested in what they have to say.

o **Actively and *actually* listen:** Don't tune out the other person and spend time mentally formulating your response instead of truly listening. (I'm so guilty of this one.) Authentically listen, and then pause if need be to gather your thoughts.

o **Know your biases:** This one can be difficult, but if you've done some inner work and are relatively self-aware, you're going to know your biases and preconceived notions. Make sure you're filtering the conversation to exclude those biases and preconceived notions. Are you only listening for what you want to hear? Only positive things? Only negative things so you can mount a defense? That will help you take in what the other person is saying rather than having an immediate reaction and automatically disagreeing or disengaging.

o **Don't gaslight:** If someone shares with you their personal experience, don't deny what happened or tell them that what they are feeling isn't valid. Don't play devil's advocate. People's personal experience is not up for debate.

o **Don't tone police:** Don't tell someone that their message would be better received if they phrased it a different way or used a different tone. This is the classic, "More people would listen to you if you said it nicer." While many would say that you get more bees with honey, you can still maintain the line of advocating for what you need while not policing your peer's tone.

o **Maintain eye contact:** Not only does maintaining eye contact show the other person that you're listening, but it also can help you pay closer attention. If you're not visually focused on the person, your eyes and mind can wander, and you'll tune out on the conversation. Don't miss out on important information and body language!

▪ **Try It Out**: Start practicing these listening skills in lower-stakes conversations and contexts. Out to coffee with a friend? Work on not interrupting and keeping consistent eye contact. Chatting with a co-worker? Ask questions to show that you're interested in what they are saying, and practice active listening (i.e., don't tune out and think about what you're going to say next instead of hearing the other person). Strong listening skills are all about practice, so if you can get in the habit of working on these skills when it's not a stressful or emotionally charged situation, you'll be better prepared for when emotions may be running high.

Other Important Components for Successful Communication

There are a few other components that will set you up for communication success, in addition to everything I've mentioned above. Firstly, it helps to connect the dots. Notice how what the other person is saying might relate to conversations you've had before or to specific facts that you know about the person. Seeing a pattern of behavior, emotions, or reasoning may help you communicate better in the present moment. And it will allow you to be more perceptive and gain a better understanding of what's being addressed.

Secondly, don't just take things at face value. Employ some critical thinking and try to make inferences that go beyond what the other person is saying. Most of the time, there's more to the story than what things initially seem, so go deeper to uncover what's really going on.

Maybe you have a sibling who you're ordinarily very close to, but they seem apathetic when it comes to your wedding. You ask them about it, and they respond by apologizing and saying they are incredibly busy at work. But you know that they've had a demanding job for years, and yet they've always made time for you before and been interested in what you've got going on. In this situation, you don't want to push someone to talk about something they're not ready to address, but you can kindly let them know that if there does happen to be more to the story than just a lot going on at work, you'll be there whenever they'd like to talk.

Thirdly, as psychotherapist and sex therapist Jesse Kahn from The Gender & Sexuality Therapy Center explains, getting clarification on the message is also important. "When you're communicating, take a moment to practice clarifying. Try 'This is what I hear you saying. Is that accurate? Is there anything I'm not understanding or that you want to clarify?' This can slow down the communication process as well as name and clarify any assumptions the listener is possibly (and unknowingly) adding."

And last but certainly not least, you've got to give and be able to receive feedback. No two people are alike, and that means we all communicate in different ways. Part of building a solid foundation for your relationship with your partner is learning to communicate with each other. For example, in my own relationship, I like to get everything out on the table the minute I feel the need, which means that I'm often initiating important or emotional conversations at the worst times. My husband has pointed out that I could use some work on my timing so that I initiate these conversations at better times when both parties will be mentally and emotionally equipped to have them. On the flip side, I've pointed out that he'll sometimes miss the actual message if he feels like I've brought something up at an inappropriate time, but just because he doesn't love *how* a message was presented doesn't mean he gets to ignore the message.

For anyone with whom you engage in conversation regularly, especially your partner, you must give and receive feedback to communicate more effectively going forward.

Taking in all these skills and components of effective communication can feel overwhelming *(believe me, I know!)*. So, if you've got a big, uncomfortable talk on the horizon, it's not a bad idea to write out what's essentially a script for the conversation. Before you sit down for it, lay out your speaking points, try to anticipate what the other person will say, and prep yourself for responses. If need be, you may even go so far as to practice what you'll say in advance. The key to successful communication is making your message clear and concise and delivering it with confidence. Whatever you need to do to achieve that is what you need to focus on first.

When Therapy Helps

The best way to make sure that your communication skills are on point for wedding planning is to focus on those skills *before* you're planning the wedding. Communication is key in any relationship (married or not), and couples must learn how to communicate with one another to have a solid foundation for that relationship. If you and your partner don't feel equipped to assess and improve those skills on your own, counseling/therapy is a great way to achieve that.

Jesse Kahn confirms that starting counseling early on is key – you want to build and strengthen your relationship before you get into a place of tension. Think of it as preventative counseling. A therapist or counselor can teach you and your partner communication skills and facilitate a space for the two of you to really listen and hear each other. One of the keys to successful communication is that both parties feel heard. Then you can take what you've learned back home and hopefully be stronger communicators when faced with any kind of conflict (and planning a wedding).

I know there is still a stigma around mental health and seeking help from therapists and counselors (which is another topic for another day), but everyone can benefit from therapy. Don't wait until you're on the brink of something terrible before you start. Also, you must admit what you don't know. Jesse also points out that many people grow up without examples of healthy relationships, yet society expects us to know how to cultivate them. Our society doesn't teach people how to listen, be heard, or build long-lasting, intimate relationships, so you've got to learn those things somewhere. It shouldn't be looked down upon to seek that information and those skills from a professional.

Looking for advice on how to find a couple's therapist and make the most of your sessions? I suggest considering these few things before you start:

- Ask for therapist recommendations from friends and family. With things being more virtual these days, your therapist doesn't necessarily have to be local.
- Assemble a list of questions to ask prospective therapists to help you and your partner find the right fit.
- Gather your thoughts so you can convey to prospective therapists what topics are a priority for you to cover.
- Set expectations with your partner as to how each of you will conduct yourselves during sessions. Commit to listening to each other and reserving judgment.
- Plan to have recap sessions at home so that you and your partner can dive deeper into what was discussed during your sessions or complete any assignments your therapist gave you.

Boundaries and Assertiveness

A very necessary skill in wedding planning is establishing boundaries and confidently asserting yourself and those boundaries. Being assertive means standing up for yourself and communicating your opinions, feelings, wants, and needs in a confident, direct, and honest manner. Studies have shown that people can improve their relationships by being more assertive. And believe me, you're going to need that skill to tackle a wedding.

I've said it before, and I'll say it again, wedding planning will be at least somewhat stressful, so you've got to have a plan for how to manage that stress. Setting boundaries is one way to do that. If you don't want your parents calling you every day asking for updates on wedding planning, *tell them.* If they want to be hands-on, consider setting up a recurring call every other week where you can give them relevant information. Then make sure that you stick to that plan and don't give in to discussing the wedding every time you talk.

> **Sample script**: "Hi _____ and _____. Jonathan and I are delighted that the two of you are so excited about our wedding. We're trying our best to make sure that wedding planning doesn't take over our lives, so it would be great if we didn't have to talk about it every time we chat with you. We promise to let you know when we have any updates for you!"

Boundaries with Your Partner

You will need to be assertive with your partner when expressing what you need from them during the planning process. Maybe you like planning and want to handle most things yourself, but you want to make sure that the wedding also reflects what's important to your partner. Tell them that and ask them to be involved where it counts. On the other hand, if you're concerned about carrying most of the wedding planning load yourself and don't have the bandwidth for that, talk to your partner and develop a game plan. In that situation, I highly recommend assigning specific tasks to each person, depending on their strengths or interests. For example, you might be a total foodie, and music might be the end all be all for the wedding for your partner. In that case, you handle researching and collecting proposals from caterers while your partner does the same for bands or DJs. Or maybe you find yourself in a spot where your partner is doing all the planning and leaving you behind. You feel bulldozed – your input is being ignored, and the wedding is shaping up to be something that doesn't incorporate your wants and needs. Speak up, assert yourself, and use the communication tips I've given you to have that tough conversation.

Boundaries with Family

If anyone other than you and your partner contributes financially to the wedding, then asserting yourself and setting boundaries will be of the utmost importance in that scenario. You must be clear with the contributor what input or involvement, if any, that money gets them in the planning process. If the perfect scenario for you is that they help fund the wedding, but you and your partner get to make all the decisions, then communicate that early and often. If you're comfortable with family helping you select a venue but then you want them to butt out, explain it using some of the communication ideas above.

Even when parents aren't helping to pay for the wedding, they may want to be involved in decision-making. Sometimes they can get so caught up in the feeling that this day is for them and wanting to impress their friends that they lose sight of what the day is truly about. Or if you've had siblings or other close family members get married before you, you might hear lots of, "You *must* use Morgan's florist. Their use of roses was out of this world!" What if you didn't particularly care for the flowers at Morgan's wedding? You've got to communicate that, while you appreciate them trying to help, you want to do your own thing.

Taking an Assertive Stand

This is your wedding, and you get to make the rules. But, while I do want you to be assertive and make sure that you're protecting your own time, energy, and mental health, I encourage you to be respectful when having these conversations. Your wedding is not the time to burn bridges (though it does happen plenty), and the goal is to look out for yourself while still maintaining healthy relationships with everyone around you.

Being assertive yet respectful of the person you're speaking with really comes down to the language you're using. First, it's helpful to use "I" statements so that you're focusing on your thoughts and feelings rather than bringing up the other person's actions, which may come off as accusatory or blaming and result in a defensive reaction. Precisely what we don't want to happen.

Using empathy in your strong statements can also help the person know you're hearing and understanding them, but you're still getting your own point across. "I understand that you don't love the idea of James and me eloping, but we're making the decision that's best for us, and a big wedding isn't something that either of us wants," or "I totally get why you would want to invite your friends, but we've never met them, and it's important to us that we have only our nearest and dearest at the wedding."

Holding back and not saying how you really feel will only create a lot of hurt feelings and confusion when it comes to wedding planning. If you're new to being assertive and drawing boundaries, then a little practice will go a long way. The more you do it, the more natural and comfortable it becomes, and the better you become at being able to stand up for yourself while still being respectful of those around you.

The Art of Persuasion

More than once when planning a wedding, you're going to have to exercise your persuasion skills to achieve the desired outcome. You might find yourself having to persuade your parents to get on board with the quirky venue you've chosen. You might even have to persuade a bridesmaid that a gold sequin gown *is* a good look for her. And you might find yourself having to persuade your partner that a disco ball installation over your dance floor is a must-have.

As I mentioned earlier, when I got married, my husband and I decided that he would be in charge of booking the honeymoon. He loves researching things online and organizing the details of different options, so this was a perfect task for him. When he found what he thought was the perfect honeymoon spot, it took some persuading for him to get me on board. I was still working as an attorney at the time, so I was skeptical about taking two whole weeks off from work and not taking my Blackberry (am I dating myself?) with me.

But the location my husband had his heart set on was far enough away that to really make the trip worthwhile, we needed the full two weeks. His main argument and emotional plea to persuade me were that it would be a once-in-a-lifetime trip. "We may never have a chance to take a trip like this ever again," he said. He also reminded me that I had never taken a vacation before and fully unplugged from work – this trip was needed both as a celebration and as a time to rest and recharge. In our case, because I knew we had the money saved for the trip and didn't have to stress about that piece, his persuasive argument really focused on the emotions surrounding the honeymoon. In the end, he convinced me!

Two elements to focus on when crafting a persuasive argument are:

- **Your credibility:** If the person on the receiving end of the communication believes that you know what you're talking about (or better yet, that you are an expert in the subject matter), they are more likely to be persuaded by your words. If your credibility isn't obvious, then it's worth explaining to the other person what makes you qualified to speak on the topic to build the foundation for your argument. For example, you can bring up books you've read on the subject. When I got engaged, I immediately bought about half a dozen books on how to plan a wedding. If anyone questioned how I was approaching things, I could refer to the books I was reading to justify my position. Also, feel free to use your wedding planner as the source of your credibility. I don't know about other planners, but I'm always happy to be the scapegoat and let my clients use me to bolster an argument. *In fact, sometimes it's part of why couples hire me!*

- **Your delivery:** How you deliver your persuasive argument is equally as important as what makes you qualified to speak on the subject. You can deliver your argument with an approach based on logic and reason, or you could go the emotional route and appeal to the other person's emotions and feelings. You could present a two-sided argument so that the other person sees that you're acknowledging both sides, which also lends to your credibility because they'll see that you're not just blindly advocating for your position.

If the subject of your persuasive argument is a critical one, then it may be helpful to write down the points of your argument to prepare for your conversation. Persuasion doesn't come naturally for everyone, so if you're nervous about effectively getting your point across, some preparation and practice are always a good idea.

I truly believe that quality communication is the critical starting point (if not the solution) for many of the obstacles you're going to face when planning a wedding. If you can't express what you like or don't like, what you need or don't need, whether you're feeling happy or sad, your partner and the people around you won't know how to support you. So, start with your words and go from there.

Part Two:

Chapter 8:
Fixating on "Normal" and Other Unhelpful Lines of Thinking

Hint: There's no such thing as "normal"

What You'll Learn:

- There is no "normal" when it comes to wedding planning. And trust me when I say that because I've seen it *all*.

- Sometimes monitoring your inner dialogue is just as important as being mindful of what you say out loud to others.

- Finding better ways to understand big emotions can help set you up for success in your marriage and life—not just in wedding planning.

Several months into the wedding planning process with one of my couples, Anna and Joe, I started getting copied on a flurry of emails with Anna's parents about flowers. Her mom LOVED flowers, was an amateur gardener herself, and had a lot of strong opinions when it came to flowers for Anna and Joe's wedding.

Anna and Joe, on the other hand? Well, they couldn't have cared less. So, when I began seeing all of these emails back and forth between Anna and her mom, I knew that it was taking things outside of Anna's comfort zone and consuming a lot of brainpower (and time) on something she had no interest in. A day or two later, I got an email from Anna asking if we can meet up because she was starting to feel super overwhelmed and just wanted to get a handle on everything.

We grabbed lunch, and Anna quickly confessed that she just wanted to vent, which, for the record, is totally okay with me. I always tell my couples that if they are getting hung up on something or starting to feel really stressed to please reach out to me. I know how to talk them through seemingly impossible situations, and I hate the idea of my couples at home, just stewing in their own stress and anxiety. 99% of the time, my couples feel better after getting a chance to talk it out. *Don't we all?*

As I had anticipated, the emails and conversations with Anna's mom about flowers had sent her over the edge. But more than that, her reaction to her mom's extreme focus on flowers had her questioning her own behavior. "Why is this stressing me out so much?" "It's JUST flowers; why am I getting so worked up over this?" "This can't be normal to feel so overwhelmed by something as silly as flowers."

The first piece of advice I gave Anna was if flowers are important to her mom, not important to her, and her mom has the budget to be a little "extra," then let her. That was a lesson in picking your battles, and if someone wants to do something nice for you and you don't have strong opinions on it, then let them. But the second piece of advice is something I found out after the wedding had really stuck with Anna. And that was the idea that everything you feel and experience during the wedding planning process is "normal." People before you have gone through it. People after you will go through it. And you shouldn't feel so alone or isolated, nor should you question the rationality of your behavior and the behavior of others. In the wedding planning process, it can be helpful to envision yourself on the road with every other couple who is currently on this same journey and those who have come before you. Know you'll get through it—and that it's okay to ask for help.

So, why did being told that what she was experiencing was normal give Anna so much relief? According to Jesse Kahn, psychotherapist and sex therapist from The Gender & Sexuality Therapy Center, people take comfort in finding out that they're "normal." When people are told that they're NOT normal, they feel like something is wrong with them or that they're dysfunctional. That leads to feelings of loneliness and isolation. No one wants to feel like an outcast. Almost anyone that feels less-than-normal comes with these shared experiences and feelings.

"Normal" isn't a word that many therapists or psychiatrists like to use because it's practically impossible to define. What's normal versus abnormal depends on the individual. It depends on the circumstance, and it depends on context and culture, among a lot of other things. Behavior that is normal or acceptable in one situation may not fly in another. Behavior that meets one family's or one community's norms or standards may not be tolerated in another. As Kahn puts it, we're all normal and not normal, so there really is no "normal."

I'm of the mindset that planning a wedding pretty much gives you a free pass when it comes to most behavior being "normal." Now, don't get me wrong, I'm not saying it's ok to treat people like trash or turn into a monster when you start planning a wedding (there's still a level of kindness and grace people should maintain no matter the circumstances), but if you get into a tiff with your parents about them wanting to host an enormous welcome party the night before the wedding, you're allowed that.

If you're still not convinced that you're not alone when it comes to the experiences of wedding planning, consider for a moment four ways that psychologists classify abnormal behavior:

1. **Normative criteria:** People are identified as acting abnormally when they act in ways that are unlike how most people act or are not what people expect. Do you think anyone keeps a level head for 100% of the wedding planning process? *I know I didn't.* You are not abnormal. What you are is *human.*

2. Subjective criteria: Sometimes, we identify our own behavior as abnormal—we think that what we're feeling or how we're behaving is somehow different from what other people are doing. Everything you're feeling and experiencing during the wedding planning process is what *everyone* goes through when planning a wedding. See, you're not abnormal!

3. Maladaptive criteria: Under these criteria, you must ask yourself whether your conduct helps you to survive and function successfully in society. Getting married is a common occurrence in a lot of places. In fact, the wedding industrial complex will have you believe that getting married is a rite of passage—though marriage is not for everyone and people shouldn't feel pressured to tie the knot—and so the behavior that goes along with it is needed to achieve this almost societal goal. All of the ups and downs are simply part of this process of getting married. Once again, not even close to abnormal!

4. Unjustifiable or unexplainable criteria: People can act in ways that those around them can't explain or that you can't justify. Suppose you're absolutely convinced that your wedding planning experience somehow makes you weird or unusual or abnormal. In that case, this category of criteria is probably the one you'll point to in order to prove me wrong. But to that I say, you're planning a wedding! What better reason is there to explain and justify why you're feeling/acting/behaving the way you are?! Believe me; you are not abnormal. *I swear.*

I know I've taken a somewhat light-hearted approach to this internal struggle of normal versus abnormal, and I realize that it can be a huge challenge for many people. Many individuals are planning a wedding for the first time, and the emotions and experiences that come with it can be surprising. You may find your own behavior off-putting, and you may find the behavior of others unusual. What you are going through is so commonplace and so "normal," and I hope you can take comfort in the fact that you are not at all alone in this experience.

Unhelpful Thinking Patterns

My therapist describes cognitive-behavioral therapy (often referred to as CBT) as an approach to psychotherapy and talk therapy that's framed in more colloquial terms rather than formal academic and scientific-like language. One of its focuses is on changing our thinking patterns. There are many unhelpful thinking patterns that couples may experience during the wedding planning process. It's helpful to know what those patterns are so, when they happen, you can recognize them, name them, and try to shift your thinking.

> **Catastrophizing and minimizing:** Taking a situation and making a bigger deal out of it than it is (catastrophizing) or not giving the situation the significance it deserves (minimizing). For example, let's say you're in the phase of wedding planning where your invitations are out, you're starting to get RSVPs back, and you get a couple of "no" RSVPs in a row. Catastrophizing is engaging in the line of thinking that *everyone* will RSVP "no" to the wedding, no one will come, and it will be a terrible day. See how that works? Basically, one thing turns into this downward spiral that is purely emotional and not fact-based. An example of minimizing is looking at the weather reports the Monday before your outdoor tent wedding, seeing a high chance of rain for the weekend, and refusing to discuss a rain plan because the forecast "is not a big deal" – you'd rather address it the day before the wedding when you know the forecast is certain.

> **Over-generalizing:** Like catastrophizing and jumping to conclusions (described below), over-generalizing happens when you establish broad facts based on one event when you don't have the data to come

to such a conclusion. For example, a couple starts to look at wedding venues and finds out that one wedding venue doesn't have any Saturdays open in the months the couple was interested in. Then, the couple starts to panic and rushes to judgment that *no* venues will have Saturdays open in the months they want. That's over-generalizing. Without seeing a handful of venues and having actual data that many places are booked up, the couple's determination isn't based on fact.

All-or-nothing thinking: When I was working with a life coach, she characterized all-or-nothing thinking as viewing situations as black or white, success or failure. There was never any grey area or any in-between. But what she taught me is that many things in life are about the journey and not just the end result. So, when it comes to wedding planning, being convinced that your wedding will be terrible because you didn't get your number one choice for a band is an example of all-or-nothing thinking. Your wedding is still going to be great no matter who is playing the music. The same goes for any other element of your wedding or who is attending – the day is going to be what you make of it, and never forget the journey that it took to get there or the journey that awaits you after it's over.

Emotional reasoning: This line of thinking happens when we mistake how we're feeling for actual facts. If your wedding day is approaching and you're feeling nervous, you might convince yourself that you've missed a detail for the day. Just because you're anxious and not 100% confident that everything will be perfect doesn't mean you forgot to rent glasses for the bar. Your feelings also don't mean that people aren't going to have fun at your wedding. The people there are your nearest and dearest who came out just to celebrate you and your partner. You could get married in the middle of a parking lot (as some couples actually did due to Covid-19), and your family and friends are still going to cherish being there.

Using "should" or "must" language: Using these terms makes things definitive when they don't have to be and puts pressure on you to succeed. Think about reframing your words to "I have the option to" rather than "I should." For example, you're better served by reframing "I should have menus printed for every place setting" to "I can have menus printed for every place setting if I end up having time to get that done." Take the pressure off! There aren't a whole lot of "musts" when it comes to getting married other than having someone there to legally marry you (and even then, you could still make it official on a different date).

Labeling: Placing negative labels on ourselves and others is never helpful. For a long time, my internal dialogue when things weren't picture-perfect would always default to "I'm a mess." But am I really a mess, or am I just frustrated by a particular situation? And who does it serve to label myself that way? In case you were wondering, the answer is no one. The same goes for you and your wedding! If wedding planning has you stressed out, saying things like "I'm a disaster," or "I'm incapable of making decisions," or "I'm all over the place" isn't going to benefit you or anyone else. The key is to catch yourself in those moments and name what it is that's bothering you. Like "I'm overwhelmed" or "I'm having a really tough time choosing between these two caterers" or "I have so many ideas for what I want my flowers to look like and need to get organized so I can better sort through them." Getting specific sounds a lot better and more productive, right?

Jumping to conclusions: If jumping to conclusions were a video game, I'd be expert level. A dear friend of mine (also a wedding planner) and I have bonded over how ridiculous we are when it comes to jumping to conclusions. She was convinced that a client-turned-friend of hers was mad at her for something she had posted on

Instagram. (The friend wasn't.) I was once convinced that I was going to be fired by a client when they asked for an in-person meeting. (I wasn't – they just to have a catch-up meeting in person.) It's so easy for our brains to jump to the worst-case scenario when we have no facts to back up that conclusion. Thinking like that doesn't do anyone any good. Instead of making up fact patterns and hypotheticals in your head, focus on the actual facts you have in front of you and make decisions based on them. Taking your concerns about your wedding and turning them into some sci-fi or post-apocalyptic scene in a movie will not help you deal with those concerns in an effective way.

Disqualifying the positive: Negative Nancy. Debbie Downer. *First of all, why are these pessimistic characters named after women?* That aside, ignoring the positive and always focusing on the negative is not a helpful characteristic. You got your dream venue with your dream photographer and dream florist, but your top choice for DJ wasn't available on your date – that doesn't mean that you should focus on not getting that DJ. Celebrate the positive and remember all your first-choice vendors you *did* get to book.

Mental filter: Moving through the wedding planning process with a mental filter is like going around with blinders on to certain things. Similar to some of the other lines of thinking, when you're applying a mental filter, you're often ignoring the positive and only seeing the negative or paying attention to some realities and not others. You might choose to see only the stress and anxiety of planning a wedding and forget how wedding planning gives you the opportunity to bond more with your partner, family, and friends who are all involved in the process with you. As tough as wedding planning can sometimes be, there are also beautiful moments that it produces as long as you keep an open mind to be able to recognize and appreciate them.

Personalization: Accepting blame for something that wasn't totally your responsibility or fault. For example, if you have a friend who can't come to your wedding because you've opted not to have kids at your wedding and they don't have someone to take care of their child that night, you might feel guilty for having a "no kids" policy because it's resulted in your friend not being able to attend. But it's not your fault for establishing a guideline for *your* wedding that will make your wedding more enjoyable for *you*, and it's certainly not your fault that your friend can't find childcare for the night. Don't blame yourself for circumstances that are outside of your control.

The first step in changing your behavior and altering your thought patterns is to be able to recognize, acknowledge, and name when you're engaging in one of the foregoing ways of thinking. If they mindlessly keep happening without your awareness, then they'll only persist. For me, being able to recognize and then name when I'm jumping to conclusions has been immensely helpful in preventing a negative thought spiral.

PRO TIP: Change doesn't happen overnight, and especially if you tend to fall into these patterns in your life beyond wedding planning, you're going to need to spend some time deprogramming.

If you're into the idea, working with a therapist can be incredibly helpful with that journey. But for the time being, awareness of these thought patterns is key to identifying this line of thinking in yourself and those around you while you're planning a wedding. Once you're able to give a name to a thought, you're taking away some of the power it has over you.

"Wedding planning can bring out the worst in our perfectionist and people-pleasing tendencies. The best way to recover from burnout is to prevent it. Getting married should be a celebration. Going into the process with boundaries, honoring your own self-care, and recognizing that your wellbeing is a priority are critical."

– Callie Exas

Chapter 9:
Wedding Planning Can Be Stressful

But it doesn't have to be!

What You'll Learn:

- Understanding how stress impacts your body can give you clues on how to best react, keeping your head and heart aligned.

- When planning your wedding, be kind to yourself, be protective of your time and energy, and don't strive for an ideal that's impossible to achieve.

- Putting yourself first isn't selfish; it's necessary for the planning process. Ensuring you are sleeping soundly, eating well, and relaxing when necessary make you a better planning partner!

I always tell my couples that in working with them, I'm going to do my best to reduce their stress as much as I can, but I never, ever tell them that I'm going to make wedding planning stress-free. Because aside from your fairy godmother, no one can make that happen for you. Since that's the case, let's do a deeper dive into the impact stress has and how we can manage it.

It is widely accepted that stress has a physical impact on our bodies. Stress causes inflammation and can impact our nervous system, immune system, and gut health. Chronic stress increases cortisol levels, which then impacts hormonal balance, which in turn affects how we function each day, including how our body processes energy. Stress makes us tired and irritable and affects everything from our brain to our tummy.

Given what stress does to us mentally and physically, it's no wonder that individuals experience illness during the wedding planning process. One of my clients came down with shingles when she decided to combine wedding planning with starting a new job *and* moving into a new home. A friend of mine who got married developed pneumonia on her honeymoon, a definite sign of exhaustion and burnout from wedding planning.

To put it candidly, stress makes *everything* worse. *But I assure you, it doesn't have to be this way.*

PRO TIP: To prepare yourself, as best you can, for the stress of wedding planning, it's helpful to understand what stress is and how it impacts humans both mentally and physically.

An interesting way to view stress is not as a situation but as our reaction to a situation. This explains why people aren't always stressed out about the same things. Remember your friend in high school who thrived when it came to final exams while you were at home having panic sweats and studying day and night? Exams aren't themselves stressful, but they can *cause* a stress reaction in people, just like wedding planning. I know I'm in a super minority on this, but wedding planning didn't stress me out (except for the money part). I absolutely came to life when I was planning my wedding. No surprise then that I started my wedding planning business a year after my own wedding – I had pretty much found my calling. But for most people, wedding planning causes an immense amount of stress. And we need to dig deep into what stress does to our minds and bodies so we can try to relieve some of the stress of planning a wedding.

On a very basic level, stress is what we're experiencing when we feel overwhelmed, anxious, overloaded, or burnt out. Another way to view it is that our equilibrium is off. So, what happens when we get into that state?

Hans Selye, a Nobel Prize-nominated endocrinologist in Montreal, created a theory on stress that outlines the series of changes someone experiences when their mental or physical equilibrium shifts:

1. Alarm: This is the body's knee-jerk reaction to whatever is causing the stress. In the Alarm phase, the brain wakes up, and hormones are produced to give the body enough energy to determine how it will respond to the stressor.

2. Resistance: Now that the body has enough energy to formulate a response, the internal system that is best equipped to handle the stressor is activated and must resist the stressor.

3. Exhaustion: Hopefully, the internal system used to deal with the stressor achieves its goal, and the stressor is no longer a factor. However, if the system fails and the stressor continues to be present, you become exhausted. Once you hit exhaustion, your body can no longer combat the stressor, which in turn makes you vulnerable to burnout.

Understanding How We Cope with Stress

I don't blame you if just reading about stress is causing you stress, so I want to make sure we discuss ways to manage this complicated emotional and physical response. First, let's discuss coping mechanisms – ways to respond to stressful situations. Psychologists tend to break coping mechanisms down into two types: *approach* processes and *avoidance* processes. You can probably discern from the names themselves that the approach processes are going to be more proactive and offensive, while the avoidance processes are going to be more passive and defensive. Obviously, psychologists recommend utilizing the approach processes more than the avoidance processes.

Frequently seen *approach* coping mechanisms are:

- Asking for help
- Taking responsibility for the role you played
- Viewing the situation realistically and analyzing it in a logical way
- Reframing the situation and viewing it from a different, more positive perspective
- Problem-solving
- Gathering information

Frequently seen *avoidance* coping mechanisms are:

- Avoiding the source of the stress
- Denying that the stress exists in the first place
- Distracting oneself with fun activities to avoid focusing on the real issue
- Numbing oneself with things like food, drugs, shopping, alcohol, or sex
- Reacting with negative emotional responses, like yelling, worrying, or feeling depressed

When it comes to coping mechanisms, how people react is a function of their personal resources and coping skills, as well as environmental and societal factors. Not everyone can afford to see a therapist or lives in an area where therapy is available. Not everyone has family or friends who can help them in challenging times. When you see someone react to a stressful situation in a way that you might not personally agree with, it's important to try to understand *why* the person may be reacting that way.

Many people react with anger when they are stressed out or if the stressor is causing feelings of sadness to resurface. Imagine the father who seems grumpy throughout his child's wedding planning experience – never expressing any enthusiasm for the occasion and often responding to any wedding talk in a negative way. As the child, you might start to resent your father for acting this way and feel hurt by his behavior. But what if you realized that anger was just a coping mechanism for your father? The real stressor was he was devastated that his parents (who passed away years before) weren't going to get to see his child get married. That might make his behavior *feel* different. Not only would that help you stop taking his behavior so personally, but it could also allow you to connect with your father and understand his feelings.

After all, I've seen a lot of sadness manifest as anger, so it's always important to take a step back and try to understand what's *really* going on.

Ways to Reduce Stress

We've discussed how people cope with stress mentally (which often leads to some sort of action), but now let's address how to reduce stress physically. One way to reduce stress is through nourishment. Callie Exas, MPH, MS, RDN, and women's health, nutrition, and fitness expert, is incredibly passionate about helping people reduce their stress with the foods that they eat. She recommends making sure that you are eating energy-dense meals, which include everything from carbohydrates to good fats to protein. Energy-dense meals help balance our metabolic function by making materials (like immune cells, serotonin, and neurons) that help our body function. In wedding planning, I understand that losing weight is often a priority (more on that later), but depriving yourself of certain foods and starving yourself will only exacerbate your stress and the effect it has on your body. As Callie points out, you should focus on fueling your body so it has the resources to deal with stress rather than running on empty. Eventually, you'll hit a hard stop, and your body will let you know.

In addition to eating right, getting enough sleep is key to managing stress during the wedding planning process (and, frankly, during every other time in your life). Sleep is the time when your body recharges and restores itself. So many bodily systems rely on the downtime of sleep to re-set and recharge themselves to operate the next day. Without proper sleep, not only are you not giving your body its best chance to carry you through the stress of the day, but you also won't be in tip-top shape mentally, either.

I'm not going to sugarcoat things: There will probably be at least one or two moments during the wedding planning process that your heart starts racing, or you feel butterflies in your stomach, and panic seems imminent. In that moment of fight or flight mode, there's a really helpful breathing exercise to employ that Callie introduced me to that will help you calm down in minutes, sometimes even seconds. It's called box breathing, and it's a technique used by Navy Seals to calm themselves and reduce stress. It's also super simple! Simply breathe in for four counts, hold the breath for four counts, breathe out for four counts, and again hold for four counts. Then keep repeating the process until you feel calm and your anxiety has subdued.

Not only can box breathing be in your arsenal of stress-blasting tools during the wedding planning process, but it can also come in handy on the wedding day. Are you feeling a little anxious the morning of? Close your eyes and do a few sets of box breathing. You'll feel calmer and hopefully ready to enjoy the day!

Now that we've addressed ways to deal with stress once you're in it, how about some methods for preventing stress?

Some people are well-equipped to resist stress, a trait psychologists call "resilience." There are a few internal beliefs that people can hold that make them more resilient:

- Believing in yourself and having confidence that you can handle situations that come at you
- Being optimistic and holding positive beliefs about the future and what's to come for you
- Knowing that some things are within your control

We should also focus on compassion, self-love, boundaries, and having a realistic perspective on what being happy and healthy truly is. When planning your wedding, be kind to yourself, be protective of your time and energy, and don't strive for an ideal that's impossible to achieve. Plan and create something that feels right for you and that you can accomplish.

Also, as I've said before, don't put so much pressure on your wedding to be your *best day ever.* Having tempered expectations will allow you to reduce stress during the planning process and enjoy the day so much more.

A Note on "Shedding for the Wedding"

Oh, goodness, do I loathe that phrase. It makes me sad when I have clients talk about not eating carbs or doing two-a-day workouts leading up to their wedding. It makes me angry to get emails from gyms and trainers who want to offer deals to my clients to help them lose weight before the wedding. Diet culture is so incredibly pervasive in society – the messaging is everywhere you go, and there's no way to escape it. But it gets especially bad when it comes to weddings.

Diet culture tells us that we must look a certain way to be accepted in society. It tells us that we must lose weight in order to be healthy. It tells us that if we look like this person, or eat like this person, or exercise like this person, or buy this person's products, we'll be more valuable in society. Diet culture feeds on morality and status, overwhelmingly impacting women. As Callie puts it, women are taught from an incredibly young age that their value is based on what they look like, and so they strive to achieve impossible ideals of how a healthy or desirable body should look. She explains that diet culture is a system that attacks our self-worth by worshiping or defining a value according to thin ideals through weight loss or a certain way of eating in the name of health or wellness. *At the end of the day, it's all false.*

To combat this messaging, it can be helpful to identify your feelings (and possibly emotional baggage) around food. Just like you went through the exercise of examining what marriage and a wedding means to you, you should go through that same self-analysis regarding food if it's a friction point for you in the wedding planning process.

For Callie, food is joy. It's cultural; it's social; it's comfort. She believes in a mind-body connection to food that can help us appreciate what it does for us, rather than depriving ourselves of food and viewing food as the enemy. Change your mindset and view food as fuel and something that we need to thrive, not something that we should label as "good" or "bad." She also doesn't condone diets – she advocates tuning in to our bodies and listening to what they need. Your body is always telling you what it needs—you can't override biological mechanisms. If you're hungry, eat. If you're feeling stagnant, move. If you're stuck in your thoughts, talk to someone. It can be as simple as that, so long as we choose not to resist what our bodies and minds are telling us.

In planning a wedding, you're already under a microscope for a multitude of reasons – people scrutinizing and questioning your planning choices, people constantly talking to you about your wedding, not to mention the day itself, when you and your partner are the literal center of attention. Even if the attention comes from a place of love and true excitement for you, it can be a lot. The pressure to be perfect, especially when it comes to how you look, can get overwhelming.

A lot of couples aren't comfortable being the center of attention. And a lot of people have a lot of anxiety when it comes to attire: how it will fit and how it will look.

In almost a decade of wedding planning, I've unfortunately seen diet culture invade my clients' lives on numerous occasions. I've had clients who worked out too hard and injured themselves. I've had clients contemplate a longer engagement to give themselves more time to lose weight before the wedding. I've had clients face body image issues head-on when it came to trying on day-of attire.

My advice for these clients is always the same: as a general matter, don't go into your wedding with the mindset that you have "x" number of months to lose "x" number of pounds. Because what happens if you don't reach that goal? How will that make you feel about yourself? Or, what if you hit that goal, but it's not enough? When will the self-criticism end? There is enough stress that comes with wedding planning, so please don't add a weight loss goal to your plate.

Then, when it comes to purchasing day-of attire, you want to buy something that you feel amazing in today, not something that's aspirational, and definitely not something that you'll feel good in once you lose "x" number of pounds or once you "tone up." *Because what happens if you don't lose that weight or don't tone up?* Being comfortable and confident on your wedding day is one of the keys to really enjoying that day. If you're not loving how you look, people will be able to see it.

It Really Happened:
One of my past clients had some very insightful thoughts on her relationship with her wedding dress.

> "My dress was one thing that I was very surprised that I cared about as much as I did. I was very, very, very nervous about it. Frankly, this was tied to self-esteem issues and generally not liking to be the center of attention. I was very anxious about how I would look, even though I was confident in a lot of other aspects of our planning. I'm adding this because I went through it and had a friend go through the same thing, and no one had told me this would happen: I was afraid of my dress. When I picked it out, I loved it. A lot of time had passed between when I ordered it and when it got delivered. I still

had to have it altered here and there, but I didn't take it out of its protective bag for a couple of weeks after it was delivered. I realized what the dress meant to me, that it was the most I had ever spent on a garment and that everyone would be looking at me in it. I was very afraid I wouldn't be enough for it, that I wouldn't like it, etc. I can't remember when I decided to take it out and try it on at home, but I am glad I did it when I was feeling good about myself and the day or week I had had. My friend went through something similar. She was waiting to get her dress back but was already picking apart a lot of what it would look like and her worries. I told her that when her dress arrived, I was sure it would look good, that it was ok to wait to try it on, that if anything had to be taken in or let out, that there are seamstresses and tailors who could work wonders to fix things. Then I had a friend who told me after her wedding that she had to add an entire panel to her dress as it was delivered in the wrong size. I realized that when I saw her at her wedding, her dress fit like it was made for her, and I was none the wiser about the issues she had with it."

All of this is to say that:

(a) It's totally normal to be sensitive about how you're going to look on your wedding day.
(b) Diet culture isn't doing you any favors.
(c) We need to shift our mindset on how we approach health and wellness during the wedding planning process.

When it comes to wedding planning and health, Callie says that the best approach is to focus on self-care and flexibility. You can't nurture yourself by hating your body. If you want to feel good and energized going into your wedding, it comes from self-love and compassion – you don't want to go into it feeling depleted and deprived.

Been There, Done That

– by Callie Exas

MPH, MS, RDN, and women's health,
nutrition, and fitness expert

I am one of those people who LOVES planning and parties and one of those people that has always dreamed about their wedding day. When my now-husband and I got engaged, we were one of the last in my circle of friends to do so. At that point, we kinda knew what we wanted, but I was not ready for what the wedding industry had in store for me per se. The wedding industry is rife with toxic messaging about what I needed to spend, do, look like, act like, and embody in order to be an acceptable, pure, perfect bride. It was about appearances and perfectionism and people-pleasing. I bought in - we had a dream wedding straight from the boards of Pinterest, complete with a vineyard, horses, and holy matrimony - but I paid too.

My wedding took place in July of 2014, and I still remember the swift letdown that came on literally the day after. I remember the sheer exhaustion, depression, and post-wedding crash. I developed horrible periods, insomnia, and cystic acne around my jawline - signs of estrogen dominance most likely related to my stress.

Leading up to our wedding day, I should also mention that I was in the throes of finishing up my first master's degree at NYU in Public Health Nutrition while also working as a personal trainer *and* at the NYC Department of Health as an intern. *So, to say I know a thing or two about burnout is an understatement.*

Today, after completing two master's degrees and a licensure, I'm a registered dietitian specializing in women's health and hormone balance related to burnout. I help women reconnect with their bodies after years of ignoring and disassociating from them in order to achieve perfection, success, respect, love, worthiness, etc.

The thing about burnout that women often don't realize is that it's not just in their heads. It is not their fault. Burnout is mental, spiritual, and physical exhaustion. It manifests in many different ways – from an emotional standpoint to actual physiological symptoms resulting in infertility, painful periods, anovulation, acne, autoimmune disorders, thyroid dysfunction, gut dysfunction, and chronic pain.

I see women constantly trying to seek relief and heal their bodies and feel confident through restrictive diets, cleanses, supplements, and quick cures - all extremely common in the wedding industry, I might add. These tactics come at a cost, though - often sending the body into more of a tailspin.

It's really difficult for many women to recognize they're heading into burnout until it's way too late. In a society where stress, productivity, hustling, and perfectionism are celebrated, it's easy to place blame on ourselves for not living up to unrealistic standards and expectations. While signs and symptoms can run the gamut, I most often hear women describing their complete and utter exhaustion, inability to feel energetic or feeling tired but wired, in addition to feeling like they're living in a state of mental fog. Initial physical symptoms can include acid reflux or changes in appetite (either a loss or increase here). Contrary to popular belief, stress is not a silent killer. Your body is constantly sending you signals. We're just taught that it's ok to ignore them.

So, what exactly is happening here? Listen, we need stress in our lives to some degree. The answer isn't to keep yourself in a constant state of calm. This does nothing to build resilience.

However, in our society, everything is a fire drill. A constant stress state results in a lot of wear and tear on the body.

First, we have to understand the difference between stress and stressors. Stressors are external stimuli that the body's systems respond to. However, if we do not process those stressors or push them aside, stress builds up, sending the body into a chronic state of fight or flight mode. Fight or flight has many biological impacts. It starts with elevated cortisol, which has downstream effects on how blood and nutrients are dispersed throughout the body. In our modern-day, the body does not differentiate between running from a dangerous predator and having to deal with a diva mother-of-the-groom moment. Resources become diverted in order to survive. This means blood flow is diverted to essential organs only, blood pressure rises, the body shifts its metabolism and blood sugar balance, gut function is altered, the fertility pathway shuts down, and you feel like you're constantly on edge - all in an effort to help you survive when you're trying to outrun a T-Rex.

Ignoring the T-Rex doesn't work. It only perpetuates the stress cycle making you less and less resilient to stressors. What once might not have been a big deal in your day-to-day suddenly becomes a spiral. We need to face what's going on and process the stress. Recovering from burnout requires addressing the behaviors, mindsets, and practices that keep you in stress mode. Look at how your boundaries (or lack thereof) impact your ability to address your most basic survival needs - are you skipping meals to write emails, scrolling late night when you should be asleep, exercising as punishment, putting yourself dead last on your list of priorities?

Recovery starts by taking a hard look at your boundaries around protecting your energy and wellbeing. We, as women, are taught that boundaries are selfish, but in real life, they're protective. They help you show up with your A-game. They help you be productive, and happy, and healthy. Say "no" so that you can say "yes" to the things that truly matter to you.

Burnout recovery and prevention require letting go of perfectionism and embracing the idea that rest and nourishing your body are productive. From a nutritional standpoint, I work with my clients to understand how to eat in order to stabilize stress responses, balance metabolism, and heal hormonal imbalances so that they can thrive rather than just survive. It takes time, questioning, and reacquainting with the body in order to truly understand what it's trying to tell you.

Yes, you can recover from burnout, but there are no quick fixes. Wedding planning can bring out the worst in our perfectionist and people-pleasing tendencies. As an expert, the best way to recover from burnout is to start with preventing it. Getting married should be a celebration. Going into the process with boundaries, honoring your own self-care, and recognizing that your wellbeing is a priority are critical.

Chapter 10:
A Roller Coaster of Emotions

What to expect from the ups and downs

What You'll Learn:

- Anger doesn't give power; it takes it away. Learn how to understand anger and de-escalate tense situations.

- No one is going to care about your wedding as much as you and your partner do. And that's ok!

- Grief often accompanies weddings. Taking time to honor feelings of grief and understand why they are there can serve you well past your wedding day.

- The stages of grief aren't linear, and they don't flow in an easy path. Sometimes the five stages of grief move in a zig-zag pattern.

Anger

Let's face it; weddings are basically like the Disney Pixar movie *Inside Out*. Joy, Fear, Anger, Disgust, and Sadness all play a starring role, and the combination of all five emotions leads to some rather interesting behavior. But, by far, anger seems to be one of the strongest emotions in wedding planning and can often take you by surprise.

Anger is the couple having a passionate discussion about money. Anger is the parent yelling in front of everyone during the final walkthrough at a venue that the toilet paper is not up to their standards and it absolutely CANNOT be used during their child's wedding. Anger is the sibling of the bride who storms out of the room during a family dinner after announcing that the parents didn't spend this much time or money on *their* wedding. Anger is the friend who ultimately refuses to officiate a couple's wedding because the moment in which they asked her to officiate was not private or special enough.

So, what's behind all this angry behavior? *It turns out, being a human has a lot to do with it.*

Psychologists have identified the following triggers for anger:

- **Feeling depressed.** Sadness and grief, which are often part of depression, can lead to angry feelings. For their own internal reasons, family and friends sometimes experience sadness and grief when there's a wedding on the horizon. Perhaps they are reminded of a divorce, their relationship status (or lack thereof), or what they view as the loss of a family member or friend to another person. When people don't know how to express or communicate these feelings, it can manifest as anger when it's not really about being angry at all.

- **Being separated from desires.** Guess what. When people don't get what they want, they get angry. Whether it's a parent who feels left out of the planning process or one of the partners getting married who feels like they are being steamrolled by a parent who is funding the wedding, not having things go your way can be frustrating and upsetting.

- **Separation from attachment figures.** Being separated from someone you have a strong emotional bond with can be a trigger for anger. In this case, angry behavior can be seen in the single best friend who feels like they are losing their wing person. Or in the father who is about to watch his only child (not to mention only daughter) walk down the aisle.

Anger is something that couples need to be cognizant of and quick to identify because then anger can be de-escalated. Anger left unchecked can be incredibly toxic during the wedding planning process. Whether it's anger between the two people getting married or anger amongst the couple and those around them, couples need to be prepared to react to anger in a non-angry way. If anger is met with anger, things are going to escalate very quickly, and it won't be productive for anyone (not to mention that people don't really hear each other when everyone is yelling and arguing). Listening and actually hearing one another is a key component in resolving conflict when it comes to wedding planning.

If you're faced with someone who seems angry, here are a few steps for a positive response:

- Take an observant approach to the situation and try to understand what's really going on.
- Identify the underlying emotions that are manifesting in the behavior and try to address those emotions rather than the behavior that's boiling up to the surface.
- Remember that wedding planning is a temporary thing, but relationships are forever. Hopefully, your family and friends will last a lifetime, so ask yourself whether you want to respond in a way that could permanently damage the relationship.

Understanding Disappointment

News flash! No one is going to care about your wedding as much as you do. It's a fact, and it's ok, but it's one that you're going to need to accept sooner rather than later to save yourself a lot of heartache. Don't get offended by friends or acquaintances who don't want to talk about your wedding every time you see them. Don't get offended by the member of your wedding party who isn't stoked to help you put stickers on your dozens of cookie favors. Don't get offended by the wedding guest who asks you to delay your first dance while they go to the bathroom. (Yes, that happens. Though do feel free to gladly ignore their request and go on about your business.)

One of the biggest things, though, that will feel like an absolute slap in the face and is guaranteed to happen is people not coming to your wedding, especially last-minute cancellations. As one of my clients explains, "In the final weeks, days, and minutes leading up to the wedding, I was surprised by the last-minute changes, requests, and cancellations and how little it seemed like anyone outside of us understood how much effort and planning went into every detail of the wedding. My cousin decided not to come just minutes before the ceremony started." Another one of my clients had a couple drop out of the wedding just a few days before because they didn't "really feel like going to the wedding."

As much as this behavior from others can hurt, this can also be a time to practice empathy. If someone backs out last minute, it may have nothing to do with you, and there could be other issues at play. Sometimes social anxiety causes someone to agree to attend an event and then not show up once they are faced with actually going out and being in a large group of people. In other cases, maybe the person got bad news in the days leading up to the wedding, and they aren't feeling up to pretending to be happy around others. A friend of mine had one wedding guest find out the morning of her wedding that their daughter had been diagnosed with cancer. Clearly, they needed the time and space to process that news instead of attending a wedding that evening. The lesson here is to be understanding when other factors are involved.

But I get it. Having someone you care about not attend your wedding, and even more so when they bail last minute, is like a knife to the heart. My advice in those situations is to acknowledge that it sucks, feel the pain for a bit, and then honestly evaluate your relationship with that person. Is this a one-off occurrence from someone who is usually by your side through thick and thin, or is this just another brush-off in a long-standing pattern of flaky behavior from this person? Look at their actions and decide for yourself whether they are worth your time and energy moving forward.

Grief, Loss, and Mourning

It was the morning of Jenn's wedding, and she was downstairs in her parents' home, getting her hair and makeup done with her bridesmaids. Mimosas were flowing, Beyoncé was blasting from the exceptional Spotify playlist that Jenn's maid of honor curated, and a mist of hairspray lingered in the air. Jenn couldn't have pictured a better getting-ready morning if she tried.

Then, the sounds of the playlist were drowned out by the sound of someone sobbing uncontrollably. The cries were coming from upstairs, and Jenn soon realized her older sister, Ashley, was in tears in their parents' bedroom. Jenn rushed to her sister and asked what was wrong. Ashley spoke about deep fear – with Jenn getting married and starting her own family, what if she forgot about Ashley? Feeling like the wedding was taking away their bond, Ashley had big grief about her sister's big day. Opinions on the timing of this aside, Ashley's reaction is not an uncommon situation at all.

This idea of a marriage feeling like a loss to someone close to the couple might seem a little unusual, *but trust me, it happens.* In some cases, family members can view a wedding as the loss of a family member, which triggers feelings of grief and mourning. I've heard stories of fathers acting irrationally when it came to their only daughter getting married, which could have been brought on by the feeling that they were "losing" their only daughter.

Elisabeth Kubler-Ross delineated the following five stages of grief: denial, anger, bargaining, depression, and acceptance. Being cognizant of those stages might help you identify why a family member might be acting the way they are when nothing else seems to be the cause. Do note that the five stages of grief aren't linear, so people experiencing grief won't necessarily travel through the stages in the order listed below. But the hope is that eventually, they will all end with the acceptance stage.

Let's dig into each stage of grief below:

Denial: Refusing to accept what's happening. *"There's no way my daughter is actually going to go through with marrying this guy. Everything's going to be fine."*

Anger: Reacting to the situation by getting angry. *"How could you marry someone like him?! He's not good enough for you!"*

Bargaining: Semi-accepting what's happening, but only if you can get something in return. And on a higher, spiritual level, it's asking the Universe for something in return for you agreeing to do something. *"I promise to never give Allison a hard time about anyone she dates ever again so long as she doesn't marry Frank."*

Depression: Feeling hopeless and sad about the situation. *"My baby girl is getting married, and life is never going to be the same. She's not going to care about me like she used to."*

Acceptance: Accepting the facts at hand and figuring out how to adapt to the new normal. *"If Allison truly loves Frank, then I've got to welcome him into our family. I know the best way to support my daughter right now is to accept the man she loves."*

Not only do family members have feelings of grief, loss, and mourning when it comes to a wedding, but the person getting married might also experience those feelings in a myriad of contexts. It's also important to remember that feelings of grief may be stirred up by both a physical loss and a figurative one.

One such context is feeling some grief over the loss of what your life used to be. If you happen to be incredibly close with your friends, and they were your saving grace during your single years, it's ok to feel sad that you might not get to spend as much time with them as you once did. The same thing is true if you are super close to your family and now find yourself splitting major holidays and not seeing them as often. When you get married, you are closing the chapter on your non-married life. For some people, that might not be a big deal. For me, life wasn't all that different pre-marriage and post-marriage. But for some people, it *is* a big deal, and it's helpful to be able to identify whether those uncomfortable feelings that arise when you think about marriage could be some level of grief.

Feelings of grief can also arise when someone won't be present at your wedding. If a parent, grandparent, sibling, or close friend or relative is unable to make it to the wedding, you might grieve the fact that they won't be there to see you get married. To go a step further, the feelings of grief can intensify when that person can't be there because (a) they are no longer with us or (b) they are estranged. These are two very different situations, but they can stir up very similar feelings. And in either situation, you have to create space to understand what you're feeling and allow yourself to feel those feelings. *In fact, as uncomfortable as it may seem, taking time to create space to feel is exactly what strong individuals and couples do.*

Grief Is Often an Uncomfortable Guest

You might try your hardest to keep grief out of your wedding day, but wedding planning advocate and coach Meera Mohan-Graham suggests that you take a different approach: "A lot of my [clients] are grieving, and some of it is really old grief – as in the loss was a long time ago – but it's [also] a fresh loss because it's the first time you're experiencing a wedding without this person. The first thing I tell [my clients] is, 'Grief has a place in weddings.' And it's more than just a photo with the candles – your grief is invited to your wedding. It's really hard for people to feel that because I think there's a sense of, 'It's wrong to feel grief.'"

Meera further explains that she tells her clients that grief is going to be a guest at their wedding, and it's going to be a slightly annoying guest. Grief might show up when you're getting ready or during your ceremony. It may come unexpectedly and be right there in front of you without warning. She wants her clients to accept that grief will be in attendance, and then they have the choice as to *how* it will be present. Do they want to have a private moment with their partner at a particular point in the day so they can acknowledge the grief and have their partner's support at that time? Will the couple agree in advance that if at any point the grieving partner is overwhelmed, they can just leave the room and take a few minutes to themselves?

Honoring grief and the person who is missing can be difficult. Consider inviting them to your wedding in these ways:

- Leave an empty chair at the ceremony where that person would have been sitting.
- Verbally acknowledge them during the ceremony.
- Dedicate the music during cocktail hour to them and play all of their favorite songs.
- Include photos of them with other family photos.
- Mention them in a toast.
- Use their favorite flower in the personal flowers or centerpieces.
- Incorporate a keepsake of theirs into your attire or personal flowers.

The possibilities are endless and can be as subtle or overt as you'd like. Not everyone wants to have a public moment that will bring everyone to tears. Instead, you may want to have a subtle but meaningful nod to those who can't be with you. But in thinking about how you might want to incorporate or honor this person, Meera cautions folks against just generically slotting someone in. It should be a thoughtful, meaningful, and conscious choice of what you do. Not something out of obligation or what you think you *should* be doing.

Grief When They Are There, But Not

When a family member is estranged, nothing calls attention to that relationship like having a wedding on the horizon. It's totally normal to question whether to even tell them you're getting married, whether you should invite them to the wedding, or whether now is the right time to try to reconcile. Weddings have a way of making people seriously evaluate who is in their lives, who isn't, and who they would like to have back in them.

In the context of estrangement, to keep perspective, it's helpful to remind yourself why there is distance in the first place, and it's ok to acknowledge, no matter what those reasons are, that this *is* a sad situation. You're grieving (or have grieved) the loss of a relationship. You can admit that it hurts because, as Meera points out, if you don't want it to hurt or if you deny that it hurts, it's just going to make the hurt that much louder.

Is a wedding the right time to heal an estrangement? That's going to depend on you and the person or people involved in the estranged relationship. Know that you have every right to explore the relationship and what reconciliation would look like. The key with exploration is to make sure you're exploring and not getting attached to any predetermined result.

When a friend of mine got engaged, she decided that it was time to explore her relationship with her estranged mom. The exploration involved starting counseling together, but my friend made it very clear to her mom that the counseling would *not* result in an invitation to the wedding. It was incredibly smart of her to set expectations with her mom at the outset of that process.

Meera has seen grief pop up in wedding planning in another way: resentment from the partner experiencing the loss. If one partner still has both parents in their life and the other partner doesn't, the partner without both parents might struggle and come to resent the other partner for having what they don't. It's not uncommon for that partner to also get upset with themselves for having those feelings of resentment because, while they are obviously happy for their partner and want them to have both their parents in their life, it might be causing some internal pain and jealousy.

"On the flip side," Meera says, "the partner who doesn't have to cope with that grief may become worried about 'flaunting' what they have and begin to avoid planning decisions that might hurt their partner. So, now you're collectively experiencing pain and exponential emotions from all angles and feeling really trapped." In that situation, I recommend having a conversation with each other about what you're feeling, though be careful to approach the conversation from a place of wanting to discuss how you're feeling instead of wanting to make your partner feel guilty. Because these emotions are painful and powerful, this may also be a conversation to have with the support of an outside person, like a couple's therapist or an advocate like Meera.

> **Sample script**: "_____, can we talk for a minute? I wanted to let you know that I'm struggling with the fact that my _____ won't be at the wedding. I know yours will, and I would never want you to feel bad about that – that's not why I'm telling you this. It's just that I'm currently feeling a lot of emotions, and I was afraid that if I didn't get this out in the open, it would lead to resentment. Really, I just needed to say this out loud, and I appreciate you listening to me."

Feelings of grief in the context of a wedding can often feel very powerful and very overwhelming. Understanding the stages of grief and being able to identify the source of the grief can go a long way in helping you process what you're experiencing. And always remember that you don't have to bear this burden alone. Make sure you talk to your partner, a close friend or family member, a therapist, whoever it needs to be so that you can get the support you need when going through these tumultuous emotions.

Been There, Done That

– by Cara Kaufman

Financial services sales executive

Many little girls picture their wedding day. They imagine the flowers, the dress, the spouse. When I pictured my wedding day, I knew it would be a bit different. My mom died when I was 14, and I had spent the better part of the 16 years since then working towards accepting that she would not be at my wedding. I knew she wouldn't be there to help me pick out my wedding dress. I knew she wouldn't be there to hear my complaints about my in-laws or to obsess over my beautiful decor. I knew she wouldn't be there to listen to me cry over all of the minutiae that a bride-to-be goes insane over. But most of all, I knew, deep in my heart, that my mother would show up in all the ways she could.

For as long as I can remember, my father and I have had a strained relationship. He was never going to serve as my mother's replacement, neither after her death nor as I planned my wedding. As I weighed whether or not to invite him to the wedding, eventually, my fears of the potential catastrophe he could cause overrode my worries of upsetting and hurting him.

Though I had neither of my parents at my wedding, my feelings about each were very different. I was at peace with my mom not being at my wedding. I knew she would not be physically present, but nonetheless, I knew I would feel her all around me.

On the other hand, my feelings about my father's attendance at my wedding ranged across a whole gamut of emotions. Once the joy of Daniel's proposal passed, I became overcome with the fear of telling my father of our engagement. I hadn't spoken to him in over a year and was petrified of figuring out where he would fit into my wedding day.

Over the course of my 18-month engagement, I spent 17 months frantically trying to rationalize not only his attendance but also our relationship overall. I played out the million scenarios in my head for the ways in which he might detract from the day and what my responses may be. I agonized over his emotions and my emotions, the facts, and the hypotheticals.

I struggled with the knowledge that by inviting my father to my wedding, I would be sacrificing things as well. I would be sacrificing the certainty of a drama-free event and the focus on my own marriage, love, and Daniel. Over the years, I have learned that I am not capable of holding boundaries necessary in order to have a relationship with him. So ultimately, I chose my happiness and the happiness of my husband over my fears of offending and upsetting him.

Though my mom would not be physically present, I wanted to make sure that she was as much a part of the special weekend as possible. The day before the wedding, my father-in-law officiated our legal ceremony. I used the wedding band that my mom married my father with - a plain gold band. My mom believed in marriage, in love, in commitment. I wanted to carry and honor those pieces of her as I embarked on my own loving marriage.

Almost every day during the two months before the wedding, the skies thrashed with horrendous thunderstorms. While Daniel panicked over our rain contingency plan, I never once questioned what the weather would be. I knew my mom would take care of it.

The morning of the ceremony, a fawn lay under the catalpa tree where our chuppah was being built. My mom sent that fawn to remind us she was there and was working on the weather. The skies cleared and, as the first ray of sunshine beamed onto the lawn, the fawn left. My mother had done her magic. The weather on June 22, 2019, was the most beautiful sunny day any bride could ask for.

For the actual ceremony, we were lucky enough to have our two best friends officiate in front of 134 guests at Southwood Estate in Germantown, New York. Because our friends know us as deeply as they do, they were able to speak about my mom and weave in stories and character traits throughout the ceremony. Every time they spoke about her, the wind picked up. Another way she showed up for me. I received hundreds of hugs that day, but I felt the hug of my mom the entire time.

My surrogate mother took another approach to include my mom in the wedding. She made a unique speech where, instead of speaking to our guests, she spoke to my mom. She shared all the ways she had watched me grow up, all the reasons why she was proud of me, and how excited she was for my future with Daniel. It was yet another way my mom was a part of the wedding, and I am forever grateful that she had the creativity and poise to deliver such a beautiful toast.

When my mom died, it became very clear that I would have to recreate the meaning of family. My friends played that role, as did some incredible women in my life. Since I was 14, my family has always extended past the biological. My friends cared for and supported me throughout the engagement, showed up on my wedding day, and made me feel as special as every bride should. I was showered with love and support.

"No one wants to contend with heartbreak or tragedy while planning their wedding, and a natural reaction would be to ignore what's going on or pretend like it's not happening. But instead of running away from it, when you confront and embrace it, an incredibly special experience can result."

– Leah Weinberg

Chapter 11:
When Life Happens

Life doesn't stop just because you're getting married

What You'll Learn:

- Life can be beautiful, and it can be heartbreaking – and, in many cases, you'll have to keep planning a wedding through it all.

- One couple took a potentially devastating situation and brought light, love, and an unforgettable moment to all their guests.

- Incorporating the *real* into your wedding makes it memorable.

It was a sunny fall day in Manhattan. A friend and I were having lunch together, sitting outside at one of my favorite restaurants in Chelsea. I asked her how wedding planning was going for her own wedding (as we wedding planners always like to do, even when it's not a wedding we're working on). She let me know that a close relative had been diagnosed with cancer, and another had recently passed away. She said it felt wrong to be planning something that's meant to be so happy amid loss and bad news.

I tried to reassure her that feeling guilty and uncomfortable planning a wedding when things weren't picture-perfect was a normal reaction. It can seem selfish to focus on yourself and something like a wedding when sadness is happening around you. I encouraged her to feel those feelings but also remember that her family loved her and that those who were sick or no longer with us would want her to be happy and continue planning something as joyous as a wedding. But I get it; when you're in the middle of a dark cloud, planning a wedding can feel like the last thing you're supposed to be doing.

By their nature, weddings are a time that practically demands that couples be selfish. After all, they are essentially planning a day that revolves around them. So, what happens when life throws a complete curveball in the middle of it all and forces the couple to focus on someone else?

Sadly, I've seen a lot of life events complicate wedding planning for those I work with. I've had couples suffer the heartbreaking loss of a parent while planning a wedding. In that case, it's natural to question whether the wedding should move forward as planned or to think about what modifications need to be made to what's already been decided. Over the years, I've had couples recognize family members (and not just parents) who have passed away in so many sweet and thoughtful ways. Losing a parent or family member while planning a wedding can be a devastating loss, and couples should hit pause on wedding planning, take time to mourn, and decide how they want to move forward.

It's also challenging when a friend or family member gets critically ill during the planning process. In that case, it's totally normal to stress about whether that person will even be able to attend the wedding and, if they are, what special arrangements might need to be made. For example, if a parent unexpectedly requires a wheelchair, will they process down the aisle as planned or take a seat before the ceremony starts? If a family member is sick, you might find yourself in a quandary as to their role in wedding planning.

One of my couples had a parent get diagnosed with cancer during their planning process. Prior to the diagnosis, the parent was fairly in the loop on wedding planning, but the couple was still taking the lead and making the decisions. Post-diagnosis, the couple felt bad about vetoing some of the parent's ideas and suggestions, wanting to defer to their preferences a little bit more. On things that were important to them, they still followed their hearts, but on decisions where the parent felt strongly and they didn't, they went with the parent's wishes.

An even trickier situation occurs when it's one of the partners who gets sick before the wedding. I had been working with Becca and Brian for around six months when we started approaching the three-month mark before their wedding. They hadn't been responding to emails for a couple of weeks, which wasn't typical, but I also knew they were incredibly busy with their jobs, so I didn't want to bother them too much. I sent a follow-up email one morning, and while I was on another call shortly after sending the email, I saw Brian's number pop up, trying to call in.

The second I saw him calling, I knew something was wrong. I've been doing this for long enough to know that emails that go unanswered for weeks, followed by a phone call right after a follow-up email, are never a good sign. After I got off my call, I saw Brian had left a voicemail, asking me to give him a call back. I immediately got on the phone with him, and he broke the news that Becca had been diagnosed with breast cancer.

A few weeks back, she had found a lump, and they had been waiting on the biopsy results, hence the (totally justified) radio silence on their end. Fortunately, her prognosis was good, and the cancer appeared very treatable. But with all of that going on, they weren't sure what their plans were for the wedding in three months. I told them to take their time on deciding as we were still far enough out to be able to pause completely on planning while they decided what to do.

I gave them the space they needed and, a few weeks later, heard from Brian that they wanted to move forward with the wedding as planned. He updated me on the treatment plan for Becca and said that her doctor felt like having the wedding to look forward to would be a great thing to have during the treatment process. We began to tackle questions that none of us could have imagined we'd be faced with, like how Becca would do being outside for photos if it was cold, what food she could eat that day that wouldn't make her nauseous, and what her options were for hair and makeup, knowing that she'd be in the middle of chemo by the time the wedding came around, probably losing her hair, eyebrows, and eyelashes.

Becca and Brian handled those last couple of months of wedding planning with such grace, strength, and bravery, giving themselves the time they needed to slow down but also knowing that their wedding day was going to be incredibly special.

A few weeks out from the wedding, I was at Becca and Brian's apartment for the final meeting with their DJ. We reviewed their final timeline as well as song choices and overall music preferences. I hung back after the DJ left to chat through a few open items I had for them. As we were wrapping up, Becca and Brian asked if they could get my thoughts on an idea they had.

Becca had been using a system called the cold cap process during her treatments to reduce her hair loss. While it had been working, Becca was still losing some of her hair and found herself approaching the point in chemotherapy when she would need to shave her head. She and Brian had talked about it and decided that Becca still wanted her wedding portraits with her natural hair, so she didn't want to shave her head before the wedding.

Then, Becca and Brian surprised me with the most incredible idea: Becca wanted to shave her head during the wedding itself, and Brian would shave his as well in an act of support and solidarity. I'm not exaggerating when I say that I got goosebumps and tears in my eyes when they told me their idea. Becca explained that shaving one's head during chemo is one of the most isolating experiences a cancer patient can go through, and the only thing that made her look at that act positively would be to do it with all of her friends and family surrounding her with light and love.

They asked if I thought this was a good idea, and I couldn't get the resounding "YES" out fast enough, though I did tell them there wasn't going to be a dry eye in the house. They asked if they should tell any of their guests, and I suggested telling their parents and siblings the plan so that they could mentally prepare themselves. We needed to make sure those folks would still be able to function afterward, and surprising them with something so momentous and emotional might throw them for an emotional loop.

We decided that the best timing for the head-shaving would be following cocktail hour, right before their first dance. I shared the plan with all their vendors, not only so they'd be "in the know" but also so they could mentally prepare (and bring extra tissues). I made sure the venue and catering staff knew so that if anyone would be triggered or upset by the head-shaving, they could make sure not to be in the room. I worked out a plan with the catering staff for being on standby to sweep up the hair quickly once they were finished so that the first dance could happen right after without delay.

In mentally preparing myself for their wedding day (and the head-shaving moment in particular), I expected things to be very emotional, especially heavy and sad. But their ceremony was upbeat and touching, with lots of happy tears being shed. Becca was moving through the day like a force.

As cocktail hour ended, all of the vendors were abuzz with nervous excitement for how the head-shaving would turn out. I can't imagine any of us had ever seen anything like that at a wedding before. As guests moved into the main space and found their seats for dinner, Becca and Brian were officially introduced and then given the microphone to say a few words. Brian thanked everyone for coming and then handed the mic to Becca, who let everyone know what was about to happen and why. She finished her talk to immense cheers from all of their guests, the DJ hit play on Chaka Khan's "Like Sugar," and Becca and Brian took their places in two chairs on the dance floor.

They sat side by side, holding hands, under matching plastic capes while their friends and family got to work on shaving their heads. What I had expected to be so heavy and sad turned out to be one of the most joyous and happy moments I've ever witnessed. Guests were chanting "Be-cca, Be-cca," while the DJ played upbeat dance music, and the smiles never left Becca and Brian's faces. It was honestly a privilege to be there for such an incredible act and something that will hold a special place in my heart forever.

With the head-shaving finished, Becca and Brian went straight into their first dance and continued to enjoy every minute of the rest of the night. I can't imagine what Becca and Brian went through to get to that moment and what they continued to go through as Becca finished the rest of her treatment. (As of the writing of this book, I am happy to report that Becca is now officially cancer-free!)

No one wants to contend with heartbreak or tragedy while planning their wedding, and a natural reaction would be to ignore what's going on or pretend like it's not happening. But instead of running away from it, Becca and Brian confronted and embraced what Becca was experiencing with her cancer diagnosis. Not only that, they invited their loved ones into the experience to share it with them. The result was an incredibly special evening that neither I nor anyone in attendance will ever forget.

Chapter 12:
What It's Really About and What to Do About It

Understanding that things are not always as they seem

What You'll Learn:

- Arguments and disagreements during wedding planning are rarely really about the food, attire, venue, or décor. Dig deeper to preserve your relationship and accept that sometimes, weddings bring out emotions, both positive and negative.

- By identifying defense mechanisms, you'll be more able to approach conflict in thoughtful, productive ways.

- There's truth in conflict. Take the time to work through planning and the big emotions that often come with it. When you find the truth, you strengthen your relationship.

- Problem-solving skills are another tool to keep with you throughout the planning process and in life in general.

It was a gorgeous early summer day in New York. The sun was shining, the sky was the perfect shade of blue, and the rumble of the train across the tracks below made for comforting background noise. I was on the Metro-North, riding back to Manhattan with one of my clients, Emily. I had been working with Emily and her fiancé, Andrew, for about six months at that point, and I absolutely adored them. They are both super smart, do incredibly meaningful work in their careers, and have a contagiously fun energy when they're together. I also found Emily to be a bit of an old soul despite her younger age – she's someone with so much wisdom and insight into life, and she feels deeply. I had come to treasure our conversations together.

On that day, we were coming back from a site visit at her venue and were chatting—partly about wedding stuff, partly about everything else in life that was grabbing Emily's attention. Emily started telling me about an argument that she had with her father, one so significant that they actually weren't on speaking terms at that moment. She and her father were ordinarily very close, and I could tell she was getting a little emotional in recounting this story.

Several days prior, Emily and Andrew had been reviewing the food menus from their venue in order to finalize their selections for the wedding. Emily and Andrew had thoroughly enjoyed getting to select pretty much anything their hearts desired for the menu. They loved bouncing their ideas back and forth until they had settled on what were their top choices to dine on at their wedding.

They wanted to give Emily's parents a chance to have some fun in reviewing the options too, so they sent the menus to her parents. In the email, Emily included what they were leaning towards for their picks and a joking note about how having fried chicken on the menu was "non-negotiable."

Instead of a light-hearted email back about how good the food looked and how excited they were to try everything, Emily's father responded by reminding Emily that he and her mom were the ones paying for this wedding and that Emily and Andrew were not going to dictate what food was going to be served. And furthermore, he was not going to have his guests eating fried chicken. Emily was caught completely off guard by her father's response, as it was never her intent to "dictate" what the menu would look like.

At the time of this train ride, they had spent a week not speaking, and Emily was so confused and hurt by her father's behavior. At that moment, I realized that I needed to offer some advice and guidance on the situation based on my experience as a planner. After all, it's not unusual for me to help my couples navigate what's going on around the periphery of the wedding planning process. From vendor selection to event design to eye cream emergencies to conflicts with friends and family, I assist my couples every step of the way.

I started by telling Emily that I was pretty sure this argument wasn't *really* about the fried chicken. You see, Emily was the youngest of two siblings AND the only daughter, so my theory included that since Emily was the youngest—the baby—of the family, her father was getting caught up in giving her the "perfect day." For people who may not have a lot of practice with expressing their feelings and emotions, sadness can often manifest as anger. In this case, I told Emily that I believed her father was fixating on the fried chicken when really, he was upset about a much deeper, more personal issue. The fried chicken wasn't at fault; it was just at the wrong place at the wrong time.

I shared all of this with Emily, and as we exited the train and walked up the stairs to Grand Central, she told me that I might be right about why her father is acting the way he is. In another breath, she asked rhetorically, "But, at what cost?" *Whew*. What a poignant and powerful question. Here she and her father were, arguing over such a minor point in the context of a much more significant time in Emily's life. It was a great reminder to always keep things in perspective, particularly when planning a wedding.

It wasn't long before the fried chicken situation passed and Emily and her father reconciled. Emily and Andrew's wedding ended up being one of the most beautiful, love-filled weddings I've had the honor to be a part of. There was not a dry eye in the house during their ceremony, and their reception was overflowing with love, happiness, and fabulous dance moves, *without* fried chicken on the menu. At the end of the day, keeping the peace with her father was *far* more important to Emily than what was on the dinner menu.

PRO TIP: Just like Emily's wedding conflict wasn't *really* about fried chicken, many couples find themselves squaring off over similar competing interests. Taking a step back and asking, "What is this really about?" can help keep everything in perspective and alleviate hurt feelings.

This experience with Emily helped me reflect on similar conversations I've had with my couples and all the "interesting" behavior I've seen from my couples' family and friends during the wedding planning process and on the actual wedding day. Things get *weird* when it comes to weddings. That may sound like a comical way to characterize what happens when planning a wedding, but it's a critical idea and something couples need to be prepared for.

In fact, it's not just those around the couple that act uncharacteristically. The couple themselves might be experiencing emotions and behavior they've never encountered before. So, it's equally important that they understand what's happening internally as well. I believe it all comes back to starting with the *right* mindset to ensure your wedding has the *best* outcome.

When It's Not All Sunshine and Rainbows at Home

Let's be real; no matter how clear you get on the emotional history you're bringing into the marriage, no matter how precise you get about how you want to feel on your wedding day, and no matter how detailed you and your partner get about your emotional strengths and weaknesses, you're still going to have some disagreements (though hopefully after having done the work in this book, the conflict isn't as monumental as it could be).

When conflict arises, Jesse Kahn, psychotherapist and sex therapist from The Gender & Sexuality Therapy Center, recommends finding the truth within the conflict. Just like the fried chicken example you read earlier, Jesse believes that conflict is often about so much more. He provides couples with the following framework to analyze themselves, get below the surface of the conflict, and determine what's really going on.

- Ground yourself by meditating or doing some breathing exercises.
- Start writing – give yourself space to explore what is happening – and ask yourself why you care so much about the fried chicken.
- At first, you'll probably write about the fried chicken, but eventually, you'll get to what the real issue is, then you keep going. That's where relationship-changing truths come to the surface!
- Once you've identified the real issue, determine why it's so important to you and why it's causing this reaction.
- Share what you've discovered with your partner to help them understand what you're experiencing so you can clearly communicate how to resolve things.

It's important to turn inward for this exercise because sometimes you are so deep in something that you can't see what's really going on (even if it's something you'd be able to spot easily in someone else). Writing will bring you this clarity, so embrace this approach when you need to dig deeper to resolve conflict.

For me, conflict leads to anxiety, and anxiety manifests as butterflies in my stomach. From time to time, I catch myself feeling anxious but not consciously knowing what's bothering me, though my subconscious seems to tell me that something is amiss. When I feel that way, I start thinking back through the events of the day, examining them to see what could be causing me to feel off. It usually doesn't take too long to identify the source, and most of the time, it's something that bothered me at the time, but I tried to just brush it off. Clearly, that event needed to be acknowledged and was demanding my attention – it wasn't going to let me move on that quickly – so in those moments, I speak my worries and anxiety out loud and acknowledge verbally that this thing is bothering me.

More often than not, that helps me calm myself, and I don't need to take further action. But on the rare occasion when more action is required, I determine the next steps to reach resolution with myself.

Defense Mechanisms

Before I even got engaged, I knew who I was going to ask to be my maid of honor. Jackie, my best friend from college, was the obvious choice. Small but mighty, she's spunky, spontaneous, up-for-anything – a nice balance to some of my more reserved tendencies.

Soon after getting engaged, I solidified my wedding date and venue and promptly let Jackie know. A few days later, Jackie gave me a call to let me know that she's in the VERY early stages of being pregnant (yay!) but that she's due two days before my wedding date (boo!). Jackie being at my wedding was non-negotiable, so I got on the phone with our venue to see if I could move the date. Unfortunately, the venue didn't have any Saturdays available later in the year, so I was stuck with August 18th and the prospect that one of my closest friends wouldn't be able to be in the wedding or possibly even able to attend the wedding.

As we got closer to the wedding, Jackie (who lived more than a few states away) started preparing to drive to Atlanta with her husband and a few others--just in case she went into labor on the drive and needed help--for the wedding. Her preparations even included having her Jacksonville doctor send all her medical records to a hospital in Atlanta in case the baby arrived while she was in town. As you can imagine, her husband was less than thrilled with this scenario. (Thanks for going along with it, Mark!)

One of the things I love most about Jackie is her loyalty, dedication to friendship, and commitment to do whatever it takes to show up for someone, even if it means possibly giving birth in a car on the side of I-95.

Despite all the incredibly logical plans Jackie was making to make this trip happen, I started panicking at the prospect of her going into labor before the wedding and not being able to be my maid of honor. I'm a planner and don't like for things to be up in the air and to have to "wait and see" how things turn out. I needed to know one way or the other and have time to mentally prepare for her not being there.

All of that stress, anxiety, and discomfort made me start rewriting the narrative in my head. I started telling myself that it wasn't smart for Jackie to risk driving to Atlanta while nine plus months pregnant, and I didn't want her to be stressed about having to make the drive. (Meanwhile, Jackie was SO casual about the prospect of going into labor in a car, which is absolutely in line with her personality.) I told myself that I needed to take the pressure off of her, so I told her that it would be better for her to NOT be my maid of honor but still try to attend the wedding if she could: the classic case of me projecting my feelings onto her. My need to know and be able to mentally prepare for whether Jackie would be there as my maid of honor on my wedding day led me to unilaterally decided to exclude her from the wedding party because then I would *know* who would be in my wedding party that day and there would be no surprises or last-minute changes.

After talking with Jackie, my other bridesmaids, and my parents, I decided that I was being silly and that I should move forward with Jackie as my maid of honor and just hope for the best. *So, I did.* In the end, not only did Jackie fulfill her maid of honor duties and dance her butt off that night (most likely to induce labor), but the baby ended up staying put for ten more days after the wedding. In other words, I worried for nothing!

When it comes to misplaced feelings or not acknowledging feelings at all, the psychological concept of defense mechanisms comes to mind. Developed by Anna Freud (daughter of Sigmund Freud), defense mechanisms are theories on how people defend themselves psychologically rather than physically. How you defend yourself psychologically can be very telling of your personality because defense mechanisms are used unconsciously. People aren't going around actively choosing which defense mechanism to employ.

Let's dive into the defense mechanisms that Anna Freud identified:

- **Repression:** Also known as the "forget about it" approach, repression is when the mind keeps something out of your consciousness. In other words, your mind subconsciously doesn't want you to remember an event or a feeling. Repression can come up a lot when it comes to weddings. This could look like a parent repressing feelings about a previous divorce and not wanting to trigger the memories of that experience by going through the wedding planning process with their child. There could also be the repression of feelings of loss and grief of a child getting married and "growing up."

    o **Do this instead:** Do the inner work to determine what you are repressing and then meaningfully acknowledge it. Get it out in the open.

- **Denial:** As opposed to repression, where difficult feelings or experiences are buried, and it's almost like they didn't exist, denial involves acknowledging a set of facts or circumstances but then refusing to accept that it happened that way. Sometimes denial even looks like refusing to attribute any meaning or significance to the facts or circumstances. For example, if one of the partners getting married has lost a parent (or has a parent that's estranged), and the other partner tries to talk about how difficult it must be to be getting married without that parent present, denial is when the partner responds that it's not difficult at all and brushes those feelings aside. In that case, the partner's brain is subconsciously protecting them from the pain of having to acknowledge how upset they actually are that the parent won't be there for the wedding. *Feelings are pretty wild, aren't they?!*

o **Do this instead**: Be honest about what you're feeling instead of brushing the emotions off.

• **Projection:** Projection typically occurs when you attach your own feelings to someone else and believe that the other person is feeling a certain way instead of you. Thinking back to my experience, I was convinced that Jackie was stressed and anxious about traveling to the wedding while pregnant when, in reality, she was 100% cool with it, and I was the one who was freaking out. I projected my feelings onto my friend to be empathetic, but really, I complicated a pretty simple situation. Jackie was excited for me, and I needed to let her make the decision that was best for her growing family.

o **Do this instead**: Be mindful of what thoughts and feelings you assign to others, and ask yourself whether it's actually you who feels that way.

• **Displacement:** Remember Emily's fight with her father about fried chicken? That's displacement. He took his feelings (probably a combination of joy, sadness, and grief) that resulted in him feeling angry and turned the attention towards the dinner menu rather than admitting what his feelings were all about. Unfortunately, the fried chicken was just in the wrong place at the wrong time.

o **Do this instead**: If you pick a fight with someone or get mad at something, ask yourself whether that person or thing is really what deserves that anger or if there's something else at play.

• **Rationalization:** This happens when you try to explain a situation in a way that people will accept, but it's an incorrect way to classify the state of things. Rationalization as a defense mechanism can appear in a variety of situations, some serious and some inconsequential, like trying to defend why you need to spend thousands of dollars on someone to pull mozzarella during your cocktail hour.

> o **Do this instead**: If you tend to rationalize things, ask your wedding planner or your partner to be a gut check for you when you try to justify unusual behavior.

• **Intellectualization:** This defense mechanism occurs when you remove emotion from the equation and approach a situation with only logic. Let's say your parents are divorced and don't have the best relationship. When it comes time to decide who walks down the aisle with you during the processional, you might decide that neither parent should walk you down the aisle because they can't walk together, and picking neither of them is better than (a) picking one over the other or (b) having them both walk with you and be miserable about it. Yes, that's definitely a logical approach, but it doesn't take anyone's feelings into account and will probably result in more hurt feelings than having an open discussion to reach a mutually agreeable solution. When we choose something for another adult, the choice is almost always the wrong one. We should give individuals the freedom to choose, right?

> o **Do this instead**: Acknowledge your emotions and the role that they will have in your wedding and in the wedding planning process.

• **Reaction formation:** Have you ever done the opposite of whatever it is you want to do in order to mask your true feelings? Reaction formation is like taking the idea of "fake it 'til you make it" one ill-thought-out step further. Religion is a rather intense scenario where this defense mechanism arises. Perhaps one of the people getting married was raised in a very religious household but over time felt less and less committed to that religion. When it comes time to plan the wedding ceremony, that person goes full steam ahead with an extremely religious ceremony that they don't really want but will prevent them from having to grapple internally with their beliefs and save them from difficult conversations with family.

o **Do this instead:** It's best to be honest, upfront, and seek feedback from yourself to find out what you truly want.

• **Regression:** Ever hear the term "bridezilla?" I'd be shocked if you haven't, and I dislike that term very, very much for a plethora of reasons. But when you think of classic bridezilla behavior, it most often falls into this category, where someone reverts to childlike behavior. This is the person who screams at a member of their wedding party because they have the wrong color nail polish. Or the person who stomps their feet and has a temper tantrum when something doesn't go their way on the wedding day (I've seen it!). Regression as a defense mechanism is characterized by the loss of mature behavior.

o **Do this instead:** Be mindful of your behavior and if you start to regress, be quick to turn things around or enlist someone to help you when big emotions take over.

If you've ever read any of Brené Brown's books, then you know that one of her big words is vulnerability—*actually opening up and leaning into your feelings*. These defense mechanisms are the opposite of vulnerability, as they are a way of avoiding your emotions from both the past and present. It is important to remember that defense mechanisms aren't necessarily "bad" behavior. In many situations, they are used as coping strategies when faced with stress, anxiety, or threatening situations, and they are something that we need to survive. But being able to recognize them and name the behavior will go a long way in helping you respond to it in a more thoughtful way.

Your Problem-Solving Toolkit

The Merriam-Webster dictionary defines "problem" in multiple ways*:

- A question raised for inquiry, consideration, or solution
- An intricate unsettled question
- A source of perplexity, distress, or vexation
- Difficulty in understanding or accepting

*There was also mention of mathematics and physics, but that definition didn't seem right for the context.

So, when you are planning a wedding and find yourself with any of the above, how do you approach solving each issue while keeping your sanity intact? For the record, we are obviously hoping for the best possible solution here, but sometimes the best we can do is reach a mutually agreeable resolution for those involved, even if it's not the ideal outcome.

If you want to go the formal route, there's a problem-solving cycle that academics have suggested is the best way to solve a problem:

1. Identify the problem: Sounds simple enough, right? You just have to recognize what the problem is. (As easy as folding in the cheese for you *Schitt's Creek* fans.) *But not so fast!* If this book has taught you anything, it's that what might seem like the problem on the surface may not be the real problem. So, it's critical that you identify the true source of the problem before you can move forward.

> **Here's how it works:** Let's say your best friend, for whatever reason, isn't able to be the "best person" at your wedding, and you're feeling a certain way about it. My guess is that, while you may think your problem is you don't have anyone else to be your "best person," the actual problem is that you may be feeling offended or hurt because they won't participate in your wedding party. *See?* Two totally different issues, and the solution

to one won't resolve your feelings about the other. In this case, the problem isn't that you don't have a "best person" – you likely have someone else you can ask, or if you truly don't, there's no requirement that you have a "best person" – the problem is that your feelings are hurt.

2. Define the problem and identify the limitations: Once you're confident that you've identified the actual problem at play, you then must establish the details of that problem and further define it.

> **Here's how it works:** It's time to get curious about why your feelings were hurt. Is it because you feel abandoned or betrayed by your best friend? Is it because you had expectations about what your day would look like with your best friend there beside you, and now that vision will have to look different? Is it because you feel like you *must* have a best person for tradition's sake? Answering these questions will help you understand with better clarity.

3. Form a solution strategy: Now is the time for you and your partner to develop a strategy to address the problem.

> **Here's how it works:** Let's say that neither set of parents is on board with the venue that you and your partner booked for the wedding. It's not ideal to go through the planning process with all the parents hating your wedding venue, so you and your partner decide to think about a strategy to show them how great your venue is. Maybe that involves scheduling a visit to the venue where you can explain to them why you fell in love with it and guide them through what the day will look like. You can add to the itinerary showing them all the cute spots in the area, getting them to see the charm in the neighborhood. This step is all about creating a game plan to address the problem. *Problem solved!*

4. Organize information about the problem: As part of the solution strategy, you will need to collect information that will help you reach a good outcome. After all, information is key!

> **Here's how it works:** A common problem in wedding planning is budgeting. Often, families have the ability and desire to contribute financially to the wedding but don't know how much to give, or parents insist that certain things be incorporated into the wedding but don't understand that those things don't fit into the budget. In many situations where the budget is creating issues, the key is going to be collecting information about what things cost so that you can present that information to anyone involved in financially supporting the wedding. Once you can show people what things cost, then the group can make an informed decision like what the overall budget is, where money should be prioritized, what needs to be cut due to budgetary constraints, etc.

5. Allocate and use the mental and physical resources needed: Ask yourself: What resources are you going to need to solve this problem?

> **Here's how it works:** Continuing from the previous budget example, you and your partner are going to need to dedicate some time to researching venues and vendors in your area to get a sense of realistic costs. Maybe you and your significant other decide to spend the money on a wedding planner who will assist you with a realistic budget so that the two of you don't have to spend the time doing that research. In this stage, it's helpful to make sure that you are using your resources efficiently. For example, if you and your partner have incredibly demanding jobs, maybe it makes sense to pay for that planner to help you rather than you spending the time yourselves.

6. Monitor progress: Are you getting any closer to resolution with your current approach and strategy? If you are spending all this time trying to reach a solution but feel like you're spinning your wheels, it might be time to formulate a different strategy.

> **Here's how it works:** Going back to the discussion above where the parents are less than thrilled about the wedding venue, if walking them through the venue and touring the neighborhood isn't changing their minds, maybe it's time to have a heart-to-heart conversation with your parents about how much their dislike of your venue is emotionally impacting you. Maybe you need to be super clear and convey how unhappy you are with what they've been expressing to you—that just may do the trick!

7. Evaluate the results for accuracy: The official definition of this step dictates that you evaluate the results of your problem-solving efforts to make sure that you achieved the "absolute best outcome." But when it comes to problem-solving in the context of wedding planning, I'm less concerned about getting you to the "absolute best outcome" and more concerned with *did you actually solve the problem in some way, shape, or form.* The quality of the outcome will vary, but if you've reached a resolution on the problem that satisfies you and those involved, I would call that a win.

> **Here's how it works:** Let's combine some of the previous examples. Let's say that your parents want to contribute to your wedding budget by paying for your venue, but they aren't happy with the venue that you and your partner have your hearts set on. Both you and your parents agree that they need to be 100% on board with the venue if they are the ones paying for it. How do you solve this problem? You decide not to accept your parents' money. Is that the best possible outcome? I'd argue no because

you and your partner will have to pay for the venue yourselves. But does it relieve your guilt of accepting money for something your parents don't approve of? *Absolutely!*

Problem-Solving Part Deux

For those of you not so keen on taking such an academic approach to problem-solving, here are some more casual suggestions for how to tackle the issue at hand:

- **Brainstorm:** First, give yourself a specific amount of time to write down every possible solution you can think of without any type of judgment or evaluation. Once time is up, review the solutions you've written and analyze them based on viability, resources needed to carry out that option, etc. Then, choose whichever one you think is the best fit.

- **Find a similar situation:** Think back to situations you've been in previously that were similar and see if there was a solution to any of those problems that worked well in the past.

- **Break it down:** If a problem seems too big or complex to tackle on its own, break the problem down into parts so that you're solving multiple smaller and simpler problems rather than one gigantic one.

- **Test a hypothesis:** Ok, I did say these suggestions were going to be a little more casual, and this one might make you feel like you're back in high school. But if you're up for a little experiment, this option, where you come up with a hypothesis as to what the outcome will be like if you go a certain route with your problem solving and then test that hypothesis, could work if your problem isn't exactly high stakes.

- **Trial-and-error:** Like hypothesis testing, the trial-and-error approach is probably best used in circumstances where your problem isn't high stakes. For instance, if your partner doesn't like the cake at a tasting, you can try multiple bakers until you finally find the one that's right for you. But if the problem is something like how best to navigate divorced parents who don't get along, you'll probably want a more thoughtful approach than throwing solutions at the wall and seeing what sticks.

- **Research:** Roll up your sleeves and hit the books (*or the interwebs*) to research some possible solutions or learn what others in your situation have done. Social media can be a great place for that.

What's clear about any of these approaches to problem-solving is that it requires you to take the problem seriously and be thoughtful about crafting a strategy to solve the problem. During the wedding planning journey, conflict that arises will often involve other people, particularly people you care about, so the end result you want in a situation like that is one where you can be happy with the outcome while still preserving those relationships.

Part Three:

Chapter 13:
It's a Family Affair

Smart ways to deal with family dynamics

What You'll Learn:

• Families are wonderful, wild, and complicated. (That's it. That's the reminder.)

• Understanding how a family functions will help you navigate family dynamics and take things less personally.

• It's important to have conversations about how involved family members will be in the planning process and make sure you protect those boundaries.

• Navigating relationships while planning a wedding takes openness, bravery, and a lot of patience.

Ah, family. It's complicated, *amirite?* If you're cherry-picking topics in this book rather than reading from front to back, I have a feeling this might be the first section you decide to flip to. Let me guess, you're deep in the planning process and are in desperate need of a quick fix for your family woes. Well, I'm happy to report that there *is* a fix, though it might not be as speedy as you hope.

How a Family Functions

Handling family dynamics during the wedding planning process can be extremely complicated, emotional, draining, and a whole host of other adjectives that aren't particularly pleasant. Family issues appear in a variety of ways, all of which I'll get to, but first, let's understand how families function. A system called the McMaster Model of Family Functioning helps identify, from an analytical perspective, how a family unit is organized and structured and how family members interact with each other. Here are the seven main principles of family functioning according to the McMaster Model:

1. Problem Solving: How a family addresses, overcomes, and resolves obstacles and challenges while still functioning as a cohesive unit. Think about when a problem arises. How does your family handle it? Are they practical and level-headed in approaching and analyzing the issue at hand? Are they able to calmly reach a solution? Or do they get overwhelmed and frantic, overcome with emotion by the stress of what's facing them? A lot of challenges arise when planning a wedding, so how your family approaches those challenges is critical in determining how *you* interact with *them* in those situations.

2. Roles: How a family is organized, specifically what responsibilities each family member has within the family unit and the behaviors associated with that family member. Suppose you're the oldest of a group of siblings and have historically been super responsible, almost like another parent; how the family views you getting married is going to be significantly different than if you're an only child or the youngest of a group of siblings who think you need to be taken care of. Knowing your role in your family's structure and identifying the roles that others play will give you incredible insight into how to handle certain situations.

3. Affective Responsiveness: How family members express and experience emotions. This principle essentially deals with the emotional intelligence of your family members. Do they experience emotional and stressful situations deeply, or do they react in a more stoic way? Are they able to communicate their emotions with their words, or do they suppress their emotions and react in some unrelated way, like anger or sadness? Being able to identify how certain family members handle their emotions will assist you in determining how best to communicate with them.

4. Affective Involvement: How much each family member focuses on and interacts with each of the other family members. If a family member is overinvolved, they are, more or less, all up in your business. When it comes to wedding planning, an overinvolved family member can be highly irritating. If a family member is under-involved, you might interpret that behavior as apathy or even a lack of love. But you've got to try not to have an emotional response to another family member's level of involvement. At the end of the day, it's not about you and your wedding; it's about how that family member functions and what their inherent traits and behaviors are.

5. Behavior Control: What rules and standards the family has set for the conduct of each of its members. Some families might have an unspoken rule that you never talk about how you're feeling, or you never talk about money, or you never talk about family drama publicly. All of these hidden rules and guidelines for how your family is supposed to interact will help you figure out how you're supposed to speak to them about your wedding and what information you can share with others during the planning process. For example, would your family be upset to know that you told your planner about Aunt Edna's tendency to drink a little too much at celebrations? If so, tell your planner anyway (because we need to know these kinds of things!) but make sure they stay tight-lipped about it.

6. Communication: How a family conveys and exchanges information. I mentioned earlier how clear and direct communication is one of the best tools for addressing a lot of emotional struggles when it comes to wedding planning. Understanding how your family communicates will give you an advantage in handling them during your planning process. I've had couples who schedule bi-weekly calls with their parents to give them updates on wedding planning because that's how their parents prefer to be given that information. Other families are happy with e-mail updates. Others are happy with no updates at all.

7. Overall Family Functioning: How a family completes activities with the other six principles in mind. So, you've analyzed your family, considering each of these six principles, and now it's time to take a step back and look at the big picture. How does your family function day-to-day in all these areas? How does your family's overall functioning impact how you're going to interact with them going forward when it comes to wedding planning? In what ways can you be open and honest with them, and in what ways do you have to be more calculated in your response?

My goal in giving you this methodology for analyzing your family situation is that you can understand why family members behave the way they do when it comes to certain things. Then that can inform how you approach and manage those family relationships. Now that you're armed with some tools for diving deeper into your own family dynamics, let's go through a handful of ways that family can create challenges when it comes to wedding planning.

Level of Involvement

How involved your family members typically are in your life will only be magnified once a wedding is in the picture. There are two extremes here. First, you might have a family that's not involved at all. Perhaps they never ask you about your wedding and don't really care to be kept in the loop. While I'm sure some couples whose families fall on the other end of the extreme (i.e., wanting to be way too involved in wedding planning) would love to have family that was so far out of the picture, for couples whose families are under-involved, it could sting a bit. You might start wondering if their lack of wanting to be involved in the wedding is a reflection of how much they care about you when it might just be their default way of operating. If you find yourself in this situation, my suggestion is to simply have a conversation with the family member(s) and get to the bottom of their lack of involvement. That way, you're not left trying to guess what their behavior means. Maybe they are simply trying to give you your space and not micromanage. Also, remember that the family member might have no idea how their behavior is being perceived by you. Simple communication can fill in a lot of gaps in this instance.

While it's not always the case, in some instances, a lack of involvement or interest in the wedding is an indicator of a lack of support for the marriage itself. It may be a matter of family not liking the person their relative is marrying, but it can also go deeper than that. Some couples have to cope with tension around racism or homophobia in their families, especially extended families. That leads to discussions about who to invite or not invite to make sure that your partner and your guests feel safe and comfortable on the wedding day.

On the other end of the spectrum are the families who want to be involved in every decision about the wedding, attend every vendor meeting and site visit, and be kept in the loop on everything. (This can especially be true of family members who are paying for the wedding.) In this case, the family's over-involvement could be viewed not just as enthusiasm about the wedding but also as a lack of trust in the couple's ability to make decisions. Or couples might feel like they're being babied, which is where family roles can also come into play, like if you are the youngest sibling. There are so many layers to all of this, and it's helpful for couples to simply take a step back and try to understand why family members are acting the way they are. It really could just be as simple as they are over the moon about your wedding. If you're the first in the family to get married (and even if you're not), a wedding can be a big milestone for a family, and parents can feel like it's their event to host, even when it's your wedding. Their roles as parents of the couple getting married are important to them, and it's helpful to keep that in mind.

It can also be helpful to note here what you can expect from family if you're *not* the first one in the family to get married. Even if you aren't the youngest amongst your siblings, and even if you don't have *any* siblings, there's probably been at least a wedding or two among your immediate or extended family in the recent past. And, goodness, are you going to hear *all* about that wedding while you're planning yours.

Everything from your venue choice to the time of year to who is being invited and so much more will be stacked up against every wedding that's happened in your family up until now. If your family skews more on the traditional side and you're taking a more non-traditional route, you can expect a lot of questions and confusion from family members who simply don't understand your choices. They'll also probably try to convince you to hire all of the same vendors they used, which may be helpful in some cases if you have the same taste or maybe not helpful at all. Depending on your family dynamic, all of these suggestions and questions might become annoying, but just know that, in general, this is all coming from a place of love and wanting to be helpful.

When it comes to family involvement, one of my clients put it best: "Everyone is very excited and very emotional and comes with their own baggage. This is both in life and with wedding planning. People will have opinions on what you are doing, what you aren't doing, etc. They will want a lot of things. They may not be as involved as you wanted or more involved than you wanted. Being on the same page with your partner before planning begins will go a long way and will act as your north star."

After getting a grasp on the underlying "why" of family behavior, the key here is determining how involved you want your family to be and how involved your family wants to be and then managing their expectations. What also needs to happen at this point is determining and then establishing boundaries. Make sure that you are comfortable with your family's level of involvement, and if they become overwhelming, set some boundaries to give yourself the space you need.

One of my couples who were happy to have both sets of parents involved in the planning process scheduled weekly calls with the parents to update them. The benefit there was that the parents knew they would get regular updates and wouldn't have to bombard the couple with piecemeal e-mails or phone calls each week. I've had other couples determine what was most important to the family members for the wedding and ask them to be more heavily involved in that specific part of the planning process. If the family member was a foodie, they would attend the tasting with the caterer, or if they were super into flowers, they would attend the design meeting with the florist. I've also found that when family desperately wants to be involved, assigning them specific tasks to handle is a great way to help them feel part of the process. For example, have them handle assembling hotel welcome bags or favors. During my wedding planning process, my dad wanted to be super involved (*Hello!* Only child, *and* a daughter at that!), which I found so endearing and adorable. He was so into helping us assemble our candy jar favors for the wedding, which turned out to be a fun way for him to be involved and a great father-daughter bonding moment as we poured pounds (and I mean *pounds*) of Skittles and M&M's into Ikea jars.

One thing for couples to be mindful of is when family members don't feel involved enough and have hurt feelings as a result. Especially for parents who haven't had a child get married yet, the wedding planning process is so foreign, and they don't know what to expect. Perhaps they have friends with kids who have gotten or are getting married, and they take cues from that process as to what "should" be happening in their own child's wedding. One of my clients realized that her mom felt incredibly left out of the planning process after seeing how involved her friends were in their kids' weddings. Once she realized this, she explained to her mom that:

(a) her 18-month engagement meant that the planning process was well spread out and so there wouldn't be a flurry of activity until the wedding got closer, and

(b) she had hired a wedding planner so that there wouldn't be as much for the couple to do.

It took my client identifying what was really going on with her mom and then having a simple conversation to resolve things. So much of the planning process is being aware of how people around you might be feeling and just talking about it.

Regret and the D-Word

When one partner (or even both) has divorced parents, that adds a level of complexity to a wedding. Especially if there is lingering hostility between the parents, or if either parent has a new partner or spouse who will be present and might also have a significant relationship with the couple getting married, that has the potential to create complexity. Questions might arise, like who walks down the aisle? Who sits where for the ceremony and at dinner? How does everyone get acknowledged or announced? Who gives a toast? Who is included in photos?

I don't have universal answers to those questions because the solutions will depend on the specific dynamics of each family, but these are all helpful things to think about if you have divorced parents who will both be attending the wedding.

One of the situations I see being asked about a lot in Facebook groups for people planning weddings is how to navigate divorced parents who just don't get along. My hope for couples in that situation is that the parents can pull themselves together for *one day* and act like grown-ups for the sake of their child, but in some cases, they can't do that. *What then?*

I received an email from a woman who listened to a podcast episode I had done, seeking some advice. Her parents were divorced, and her mom had straight-up told her that she wouldn't attend the wedding if the mom's ex (the woman's father) was going to be there. She was heartbroken at the prospect of not having both of her parents there on her wedding day, and she desperately wanted some advice.

What I suggested to her was an honest conversation with her mom. Within that conversation, I suggested that she convey to her mom just how important it was for her to be at the wedding. Yes, she needed to show her mom that she understood where the mom was coming from and why the mom had reservations about attending the wedding. But the clear and concise message had to be that the daughter would be devastated that her mom wouldn't be there.

The other thing I suggested she tell her mom was that there were lots of accommodations that could be made so that the mom and dad didn't have to spend any time together that day. For example, the mom could be there for getting ready, and the daughter would meet up with dad for a first look with him at the venue. They wouldn't have to be in photos together. They would be seated well apart from each other. She could also ask her mom what it would take to get her to agree to be there. Remember, weddings don't have to go a certain way. The bride took time to think about how to respect her mother's boundaries and include her father. While this definitely wasn't a fun conversation to have, open and honest communication was probably the best way to come to some sort of resolution.

What's This Family Drama Really All About?

At the end of the day, if family members are acting strangely and it's not obvious what's going on, you might have to dig a little bit deeper to really understand what emotion lies at the bottom of the behavior. Sometimes you might be able to identify the issue yourself with a little observation, and sometimes you're just going to have to ask the family member directly. A great example of the same behavior but different underlying rationales is two moms who insisted on a mother-son dance. In both cases, my couples were not keen on doing a first dance themselves, but they found themselves with each groom's mom very strongly wanting to do a mother-son dance. I explained to the couples that it would be a little awkward not to do a first dance but then have a formal mother-son dance, so I left it to them to decide how to handle the situation.

In one case, the couple relented and did a first dance so that the groom could dance with his mom. In that situation, based on background information from the couple and my observations, the mom's motivation was wanting a moment in the spotlight in front of all of the wedding guests. In the other situation, the couple wasn't inclined to give in on the first dance, so they pushed the groom's mom a little to understand what she wanted. It turns out that, instead of a public moment, what she really wanted was simply a special moment with her son. The solution we came up with was arranging a private moment with the groom and his mom before the ceremony, during which the DJ played the song that the mom had wanted to dance to so that she could have a special memory tied to the song.

The moral of the story is that it pays to go beyond whatever the reasoning may seem like on the surface and try to understand what's really motivating the family member.

Been There, Done That

– by Ariana Kelly*

name changed at author's request

Like most couples who have planned their weddings, we had our fair share of family drama.

I grew up in New Hampshire, Ashley grew up in Arkansas, we met in California, and we lived in New York City when we got engaged. While it might have seemed like we had plenty of options for locations to consider across the country, we knew right away that we were going to have the wedding in a coastal New England town. The bulk of our guests, about 30 of my family members who would definitely attend, lived in the Northeast, so it made sense to have it semi-close to where we live and not to ask so many people to travel far. The day after getting engaged, Ashley's side of the family immediately took issue with the fact that they would need to be the ones to make the trip. Her mother didn't understand why we would not consider having the wedding in Texas, which was "halfway" between our family and our friends on the east and west coasts. One key reason was that we would be a queer couple getting married in Texas, and I was not willing to subject our special day to even the possibility of homophobia. I also have zero personal connection to the area, nor does Ashley since her family relocated when she had grown up. In the end, her family accepted that it made sense for six adults and three children to make a vacation out of it to visit a part of the country they had never been to instead of asking 30 people on my side to fly to Texas.

When we sat down to create our initial guest list, we agreed wholeheartedly that we wanted to be surrounded by loved ones who were enthusiastically supportive of us as a couple. It was the easiest decision to make at the beginning. We knew that meant there would be several family members who wouldn't be included on the list. Ashley was raised in a Southern Baptist church, and some of her aunts had previously expressed homophobic and selective feelings when it came to their faith. She does have a handful of supportive cousins we sent invitations to who I had never met before. We heard from other family that those who had been disrespectful were disappointed they didn't receive invites, but we felt it was important to respect ourselves and not subject our love to judgment by those who didn't truly care for us anyway. To this day, we still have yet to receive a "congratulations" on our engagement or marriage from those family members. Ashley has had conversations since with those who are still stating that they simply "don't believe we are married" based on their religious beliefs. Our supportive family members never questioned our decisions on this but have tried to make excuses and defend their bigoted opinions.

From the minute my family knew Ashley existed, they have adored her. The only person I had been nervous to come out to when we first started dating was my grandmother. She only asked if I was happy and has let us know that is all she has cared about ever since. The lack of acceptance from Ashley's family has made her even more grateful that my aunts and uncles love her as if they've known her her whole life and have always very happily accepted her and our love.

In addition to the location and guest list issues, we also had a bit of financial pressure to make decisions to please my father and step-mother, who were not paying for the whole wedding, but were the only people to contribute money and gifted my dress. While my dad was mostly easygoing throughout our two-year planning journey, he did try to throw a little weight around, especially at the end when demanding he have a very specific seat at the wedding. They also guilted us into extending invitations to my three step-siblings and their families, who are perfect strangers, adding an unwanted 12 guests to our already tight list. Those 12 people never even bothered to respond to their RSVPs…

When we got engaged, I asked my two sisters and one male best friend to be in my wedding party. One of my sisters has always been my best friend, and the other I was asking out of obligation as we have had a strained relationship our entire lives. Shortly after asking, we had a major falling out. Even though it was never discussed, I mentally demoted her to being a guest, and she started telling family she would not be attending. While I wanted so badly to uninvite her after her hurtful behavior, I knew that wouldn't be a choice I'd want to look back on with regret. As the wedding date drew closer, we began to try patching things up, and I did end up asking her to do a brief reading during the ceremony.

As a queer couple, when we began searching for vendors, we knew we were looking for those who were LGBTQ+ friendly and who properly credited other vendors. When I came across a potential planner's website, I was thrilled to see same-sex couples in the featured images and inclusive language throughout the copy and contact form. Upon reaching out, the owner of the company was enthusiastic about working with us, which was exactly what we were looking for. The process moved quickly, and I was excited to receive a proposal first thing the following morning. Excitement quickly turned to uneasiness when I clicked through to see "Bride" and "Groom" listed next to our names. It's unfortunately very common for uneducated or rude people to ask "who is the man" in our relationship, often replaced with "groom" during our two-year engagement. I had been so looking forward to work with this planner but immediately felt the sting of heteronormativity. It was particularly disappointing after our previous conversation, and I immediately responded to let her know it was hurtful. It was tough to navigate as a fellow professional, not feeling like I thought I was more knowledgeable, but I thought she needed to be aware why that wasn't a good oversight to make. She thankfully took the feedback well and was very apologetic, so we decided to move forward with working together. Mistakes happen, and I appreciated that she reflected upon the incident as an opportunity to learn.

Fortunately, that was the only specific instance we experienced like that. We were careful to choose people and places that would respect our love and identities. If someone had "bride" and "groom" on their contact forms, we didn't even consider reaching out.

And even though we chose to only contact vendors we were confident were LGBTQ+ friendly on the surface, there was always a little voice in the back of our minds fearing that we could be turned away, or discriminated against, or put into boxes where we don't belong. During our planning process leading up to our October 2018, the Supreme Court ruled in favor of the anti-LGBTQ+ baker to refuse service to a same-sex couple. We were nervous this would encourage others to challenge our rights with their religious freedoms, even though we were getting married in Maine, where same-sex marriage has been legal since 2012.

When the time came to purchase a suit for Ashley, we went with a company that created custom options for the best fits, but for men only. When our consultation came, we felt lucky that it happened to be with a woman, but the process wasn't ideal. At the second fitting, there were unnecessary comments made regarding body shapes that didn't feel welcoming or inclusive.

Cisgender or heterosexual couples most likely do not have to worry about inappropriate comments about their identities or relationship like that, or being asked who the groom is in a wedding between two women, feeling like their love is less than just for being who they are.

Chapter 14:
The Id, the Ego, and the Superego Walk into a Bar...._

When pride becomes an uninvited guest

What You'll Learn:

- Humans are going to be human, messy emotions and all. Knowing what to expect and understanding the why behind certain behavior will help you take things less personally.

- Ego comes into play for a variety of reasons. Understanding and giving grace can make all the difference.

- Narcissism takes ego and pride a step further. Protecting yourself when interacting with a narcissist will require empathy and boundaries.

Understanding the role that pride and ego play in a wedding for people other than the individuals getting married was something that I didn't really grasp at the outset when starting my business. Most of my couples, then and now, would talk about the importance of the day feeling personal to them and an accurate representation of them as a couple. They want a fun party to celebrate with family and friends and want to make sure everyone feels included and comfortable. They aren't looking to necessarily impress anyone with the party and instead want to focus on making the most of this rare occasion in life when you can have all of your favorite people in one room together, celebrating you.

With that idea in mind, I focused a lot initially on making sure the wedding was ultimately what the couple wanted. And rightly so. But then, as I started to observe the behavior of the parents or family members of the couples more and more, an interesting trend started to emerge. Family, whether financially invested or not, was a lot more emotionally invested in the more superficial aspects of the wedding day because they wanted to impress their friends and other family members.

Over the years, I would notice weddings where the couple was so thrilled with how everything turned out, but the parents felt otherwise. There were the parents (who didn't contribute financially to the wedding) who were mortified by how their child's wedding was impacted due to a blizzard. Or the parents who only paid for the alcohol at the wedding and then complained afterward about the premium liquor they had paid for not being served at the wedding (which turned out to be a false accusation). Or the parents (who paid for the wedding), who were part of a culture where the absolute worst thing that could happen at a wedding is for there not to be an abundance of food, and the caterer ran out. In these situations, it was less about someone not doing their job or living up to the parents' standards of service and more about how the parents felt like others perceived them because of what happened. They were embarrassed. Their egos were bruised. They wanted the wedding to impress their friends and family and, to them, that wasn't achieved.

There is absolutely nothing "wrong" or unusual about this type of behavior or concern – a parent feeling this way is totally natural. *It's part of standard human behavior.* A wedding is a high-stakes event, and for the most part, a wedding of this magnitude happens only once with each child, so it's no surprise that parents want perfection. But there is a point when a parent's behavior can cross into the territory of being mean, controlling, or selfish and no longer taking the child's interest into account. There is most definitely a line between wanting to be hospitable and wanting to appear superior. Psychologist Karen Horney attributed this type of behavior to people whose anxiety manifested in them trying to control and assert power over others.

Specifically, she identified the following needs that lead to this type of action and that make total sense when trying to understand a parent's motivation when it comes to a wedding:

- The need to have power
- The need for prestige
- The need for personal achievement
- The need for personal admiration

Let's Make a Weekend of It

One of the areas where being over-accommodating (or even showing off) to guests has become very prevalent is when it comes to wedding weekend activities other than the wedding itself. I'm talking about things like rehearsal dinners, welcome parties, and morning-after brunches. *Wedding weekends are a thing.* I'm not quite sure who came up with the idea to host, feed, and house wedding guests for a multi-day event, but it's really taken hold.

On the one hand, I totally understand wanting to be hospitable and welcoming. Yes, out-of-town guests are spending a lot of money to come to the wedding, and it makes sense that you want to try and relieve the financial burden a bit by having other wedding events that they can attend for free. But on the other hand, these people are (hopefully) coming to the wedding because they love and care about the couple, not because they are looking for a free weekend getaway. They are adults, and they understand the costs involved, and they can also take care of themselves when it comes to navigating a new locale for a weekend.

For rehearsal dinners, I generally recommend that only immediate family and the wedding party get invited in order to keep stress levels and costs low. I know a lot of people feel like they should invite anyone from out-of-town to the rehearsal dinner, but once you go down that path, you could be throwing a mini wedding. Eighty people at your rehearsal dinner? *That's not exactly going to be the low-key, intimate dinner that will allow you to relax before the big day.*

PRO TIP: An alternative I suggest to my couples is to have a smaller rehearsal dinner, but then let everyone know that you'll be at "x" bar after dinner for a couple of hours. That way, guests don't feel obligated to attend (maybe they want to do some exploring on their own), the couple can have the opportunity to spend time with guests before the wedding, and everyone pays for their own drinks, so no one person is responsible for the entire bill.

The morning-after brunch is where I have A LOT of opinions. First, you just spent six-plus hours with all of these people the day before. Why do you need to see them again nine hours later? Second, if you're the couple, I've got to imagine the last thing you want to do after partying all night is get up early the next morning, look presentable, and have to make chit-chat with everyone you just spent the previous day with. Third, if we're being honest, a lot of guests don't want to wake up early the next morning either. I've been on the receiving end of morning-after brunch invitations, and trust me, it's not at the top of my list to attend. My thoughts on morning-after brunches could go on and on, but the last tidbit I'll leave you with is that they cost more money. I am all about helping my couples (and their families) spend money efficiently, so I always ask the question of "Do you *really* want to spend money to feed the small handful of guests who will actually show up to brunch the next morning?"

I give this same talk to pretty much all of my couples when they talk to me about who should be invited to the rehearsal dinner, whether they should have a welcome party for a larger group of guests afterward, and then whether they should have a morning-after brunch. But then I always end that conversation by saying that it doesn't matter what I think, and it doesn't always matter what the couple thinks, because in the end, what the parents want when it comes to events like these tends to rule the day because, in most cases, the parents want to be extra hospitable to *their* friends and family.

For one of my clients, the Sunday brunch was the tipping point that sent her into stress mode during the planning process. Her parents insisted on having a morning-after brunch, which she initially pushed back on. Financially and timewise, she didn't think it was necessary. Eventually, she saw how important this was to her parents and told them that if they wanted a Sunday brunch, they could take the lead and plan it themselves. After all of that back and forth, my client did admit that "the brunch was a wonderful way to spend more time with family and friends, reminisce on the wedding night, and say our goodbyes. *It was actually great.* Sometimes mom and dad do know best, I guess."

Another couple ran into similar issues with their parents when both sets of parents were adamant about having a welcome event for out-of-town guests. As is usually the case, the couple's immediate reaction was to push back for financial reasons. Did the parents really need to spend money and time on an event for over half of the wedding guests? Like my other couple, this couple also eventually relented and told the parents that if they wanted to plan something and pay for it, they should go ahead. In the end, the compromise was a casual get-together for drinks with out-of-town guests, and then the groom's father hosted a dinner for his friends and family that the couple stopped by for before going to spend time with friends.

Another related concept is overcompensation. As part of a person's need for success and superiority (which psychologist Alfred Adler characterizes as the desire for personal gain and community benefit), overcompensation comes into play when a person begins to compensate for their weaknesses but takes it a bit too far.

Overcompensation can appear in several different contexts when it comes to a wedding:

- For the person getting married who has historically been self-conscious about their appearance, overcompensating could mean losing a significant amount of weight or even turning to cosmetic surgery before the wedding.

- For the divorced parents of one of the people getting married, overcompensating could mean the ex-wife wearing a bombshell gown to the wedding in order to show off and show up her ex's new partner.

- For the parents of each person getting married, overcompensating could mean competing with the other parents over who contributes more money to the wedding festivities. A planner friend of mine was asked by one set of parents how much money other parents were spending on the wedding ceremony and reception. Those parents then proceeded to spend an equal amount on the rehearsal dinner and welcome party.

Being able to recognize when someone's actions are being driven by something deeper behind the scenes goes a long way in helping you relate to and understand that person and keep the relationship on solid ground.

Narcissism

Before I became a wedding planner, a co-worker of mine told me about her mother, who was a clinically diagnosed narcissist. At that time, I'd definitely heard the word thrown around, generally associating it with someone who was self-centered, but I didn't have any personal experience with a narcissist, nor had I really heard stories from anyone that did. My co-worker's relationship with her mother wasn't a positive one, and while she and I weren't close enough to share a lot of the details about her experiences with her mother, one of the stories she told me is etched into my mind forever: On my co-worker's wedding day, her mother was having such a difficult time not being the center of attention that her mother falsely started complaining of chest pains so that someone would call 911, send an ambulance to the scene, and all attention would be refocused on her.

As Paul Kleinman explains in *Psych 101*, the technical term for this is narcissistic personality disorder. It is characterized by "having a grandiose idea of one's own self-importance, being preoccupied with fantasies of power and success, holding a belief that the narcissist is unique and should only associate with—and can only be understood by—those people that are of the same status, feeling entitled and deserving of special treatment, being jealous of other people, believing that other people are jealous of them, taking advantage of others for personal gain, being apathetic towards others, and constantly desiring praise, affirmation, and attention."

The word narcissism is derived from the Greek mythological character, Narcissus, whose punishment for spurning a loving embrace from a mountain nymph named Echo was to fall in love with his own reflection. *Pretty apropos, right?*

I've had friends who have dated narcissists or survived relationships with narcissistic parents, so I consider myself rather fortunate not to have had much experience with narcissists, either personally or with clients. But over the years, I have had some parents of my couples who showed some of those characteristics. Let me be clear; I'm not here to diagnose anyone. I only want to help couples understand the behavior of those around them who might show some narcissistic qualities from time to time.

Narcissism may present itself in the parent who insists on having a parent dance at the reception out of a desire to be the center of attention and to feel "honored" in some way. I've seen it first-hand, even after the couple has expressed a desire not to even have a first dance. Or it can show up in the family member who refuses to pay for a component of the wedding unless it is made clear to all the guests that said family member is paying for that component. This scenario highlights the narcissist's need for recognition and praise.

When it comes to wedding planning, the narcissist in your life may take one of two approaches. Firstly, they might become suddenly absent from the whole process; unable to handle the fact that the couple is the center of attention, the narcissist will become detached and removed, feeling inconvenienced by the fact that the couple now has other things to focus on. In addition, classic narcissistic behavior involves refusing to listen and having no desire to care about or understand others' needs.

In other cases, the narcissist may play the martyr, having a hand in everything, being overly helpful, and then proclaiming how exhausted they are and how no one appreciates everything they are doing. This can also lead to some child-like behavior when ignored, like throwing tantrums, pouting, or sobbing. *Yes, I've seen grown adults do this, and I know you have too!*

Looking back at all of my weddings, sure, there have been some overzealous parents who wanted everything to be perfect for their child or who wanted to impress their friends with a stunning soirée, but one parent, in particular, stands out as exhibiting multiple signs of narcissistic behavior. From the background given by the couple about this parent, he was the patriarch of the family. Always presiding over family gatherings, always demanding that his kids attend holidays at his home and not with their partners' families. He was clearly the boss.

Knowing the kind of role that the father would want to have in the wedding had he paid for it, the couple chose to fund the wedding themselves (wise move!) in order to maintain control. Throughout the wedding planning process, multiple conversations happened about the father wanting to be honored at the wedding and having some kind of involvement in the day. The couple eventually gave in to a father-daughter dance to appease him. And he did end up paying for one component of the wedding – the flowers, though after the wedding, he contacted the florist about something that he wasn't happy with and ended up getting a partial refund for his ONLY financial contribution to the wedding.

It can be helpful to identify whether any challenging individuals in your life are narcissists so that you can know how best to handle and interact with them.

Take a peek at this list of thirteen traits common to narcissists:

- Self-centered and self-absorbed (believes they should be the center of attention)
- Entitled (believes they are deserving of special treatment without actually having earned said special treatment)
- Puts people down and acts like a bully
- Demanding
- Generally distrusts and is suspicious of others
- Perfectionist
- Superiority complex
- Constantly seeking approval, praise, and recognition from others
- Lacks empathy
- Lacks remorse
- Compulsive tendencies (gets obsessed with details)
- Addictive tendencies
- Detached from emotion

Here are some helpful techniques for dealing with a narcissist:

Empathy: The first is empathy – understanding the other person's experience by putting yourself in their place by trying to grasp what they are going through mentally and emotionally. To clarify, this practice of empathy does NOT mean that you have to agree with this other person's behavior or accept this person's behavior as acceptable. Rather you use empathy as a tool to see what they see. For example, if you have a narcissistic parent who is suspicious of your partner's motives for marrying you, empathy will help you see why that suspicion manifests in aggressive or angry words or behavior.

Self-Assertion: It is also important for you to stand up for yourself when dealing with a narcissist. Be vocal about your needs, how their negative behavior is impacting you, and the fact that their actions are unacceptable. The key here, though, is to be assertive in these interactions but not be angry or aggressive, as that will likely result in an unproductive conversation.

Boundaries: With narcissists, establishing and enforcing boundaries will also be crucial. For yourself, determine what role you are going to allow this person to have in your life and how you can interact with them in a way that protects your energy and mental health. Then, either communicate those ground rules to the person or be sure to let them know any time they've crossed a boundary. Consistency and clear communication will be vital to maintaining these boundaries and hopefully having them respected.

If you believe that there's a family member or friend exhibiting narcissistic behavior during the planning process, it may be helpful to seek the counsel of a therapist in order to understand the other person's behavior and acquire tools for how to handle and interact with that person.

Chapter 15:
Your Wedding Party

It's not like the movies, so here's what to know

What You'll Learn:

- Your wedding party doesn't have the same expectations about your wedding as you do. Communicate early and often, and you'll have a more engaged and happier group.

- Having grace for someone in your wedding party going through a difficult time can sometimes be the best way forward.

Can I be brutally honest for a second? When I have a couple tell me that they aren't having a wedding party, I breathe a sigh of relief. Not only because I'm relieved that I won't have to try to wrangle a dozen super pumped (sometimes already drunk) individuals and get them down the aisle (herding cats, anyone?), but also because I know that it's probably going to save my couple a lot of headaches as well.

In most cases, the wedding party is comprised of very close family and friends who were significant to the couple at different points in their lives. There's the person they've known since childhood, the one or two best friends from college. Sometimes it's the people who they've grown super tight with since entering adulthood, and then a sibling or two. Very rarely are all the members of the wedding party *themselves* close friends, which can sometimes make for awkward interactions and, at the extreme end, conflict.

I've heard more than one story about a member of the wedding party having to be "fired" before the wedding because they were causing too much drama and just couldn't get along with the rest of the group. Or the member of the wedding party who refuses to use the hairstylist and makeup artist that the person getting married is paying for and hires their own team because whoever the person getting married is using "just aren't good enough." As one woman I interviewed for this book so eloquently put it, "In real life, bridesmaids aren't like the movies. Chances are your friends won't be as invested as you'd like them to be. If you have movie-type expectations, you might be disappointed."

She's right that your friends and family aren't going to be as into the wedding as you are. They might not understand why certain things are important to you and your partner and might not show the level of support that you're hoping for. In addition, being a member of the wedding party can bring up a lot of emotions for people. Depending on their maturity level, they might not know how to react to someone else being the center of attention, or they might be jealous. If they're perpetually (or even currently) single, your marriage could dredge up feelings of inadequacy. One woman I talked to told me about her maid of honor, who became so distant by the time of the wedding that they were barely on speaking terms. It turns out that the engagement made this maid of honor take stock of her life, and she realized she wasn't so thrilled with where she was. *Totally understandable.*

Grace Is Power

When you find yourself in a position like that with a member of the wedding party, it's important to remember to show some grace towards that person to preserve the relationship rather than writing it off. *Hold space and honor that person's feelings.* Try to engage with them and understand where they are coming from rather than saying something like, "This is my day, and you need to get your act together. Stop behaving like this." Imagine how much more productive it would be to say, "It seems like this wedding is stirring some things up for you. Do you want to talk? Do you need some space?" Approaching it delicately, rather than just being like, "Well, get on board, or you're out," is going to be a more sensitive and mature way to handle the situation. But do remember that you can't control the outcome and, at least for the time being, will have to accept wherever the conversation leads you with your friend or family member.

Another example would be if a member of the wedding party can't make it to one of the pre-wedding activities, like a shower. It is totally valid if you're feeling sad about their absence, but don't bottle up those feelings so much that they morph into anger or resentment. An unhelpful response to their absence would be, "Fine; it doesn't matter if you're there or not. The party is about us and not you anyway." A more productive response would be, "I'm really bummed you won't be able to make it to the party. It really would have meant a lot to me for you to be there. Is there any way you can make it happen?"

When It's Not a Party

It's already been established that I am a *big* fan of open and honest communication. Talk to your wedding party up front about why you chose them to be part of the wedding party, what your expectations are of them in terms of traditional wedding party duties, and what your expectations are in terms of their financial commitment. Then, be understanding and gracious if someone has to turn the responsibility down because they don't have time to plan a party for you or help with wedding planning or because they can't afford everything that being part of the wedding party entails. During the wedding planning process, if a conflict arises, *talk about it.* Don't bottle it up and just complain about the person behind their back.

Another facet of having a wedding party that gets sticky is, by virtue of just having a wedding party, you're having to pick certain people, attach a level of importance to them, and exclude others. How do you decide who to ask to be in your wedding party? What if someone was your best friend growing up, but you haven't been close in recent years? Do you opt not to include them and instead ask someone who you've known for a much shorter time but who has been there for you through the ups and downs of your adult life? *I get it – it's complicated.*

Think about it; a wedding party forces you to rank the people in your life. Even amongst the people in the wedding party, you must assign them a value (if you so choose). Like naming someone maid of honor, man of honor, person of honor, best man, best woman, best person. And then if you're wedding party is standing up with you during the ceremony, you've even got to rank them then! Because not everyone can stand next to you, and someone is going to be left standing all the way on the end. Just some food for thought.

If the idea of ranking your friends and family in this way makes you uncomfortable, but you still want to have a wedding party that stands up with you during the ceremony, then one way to avoid assigning supreme importance to one or two people is to skip the person or honor or best person designation. If you want to avoid ranking people even more and are ok with not having a wedding party to stand with you during the ceremony, you can get those people involved on the wedding day in a myriad of other meaningful ways. You can invite them to get ready with you that day. You can include them in the portrait session with your photographer. You can have them do a reading during the ceremony. You can ask them to give a toast during the reception. There are plenty of ways to make people feel important and included that doesn't require them to be on display during the ceremony with the insinuation that "here are my most favorite people in the world."

Also, people can get so weird about being in the wedding party when it comes to how they're asked to be in it. Things have gotten so over the top with wedding party proposals, and now they are supposed to be as exciting as the initial proposal between the couple themselves. There is definitely not a dearth of "Will You Be My Bridesmaid?" gift box ideas on Pinterest. So, what happens when a member of your wedding party refuses to be part of the wedding because they don't feel like you asked them in a special way?

This happened to one of my couples when they had a FaceTime call with a friend overseas to ask her to be part of the wedding. She ultimately refused because she was so offended that the couple didn't call her in private (there was someone else in their apartment during the call).

There are countless stories of wedding party members behaving questionably, and a lot of that behavior probably stems from the entitlement that a member of the wedding party feels as a result of their designation as such. They feel like they have an incredibly important role in the wedding and deserve special treatment. But note that they haven't actually done anything to earn that role, other than be a friend or family member of one of the people getting married.

I've experienced a member of the wedding party not-so-politely insisting at the end of the night that I needed to pack up all of the flowers in their vases for the couple to take home. Now, if you've never hired a florist before, you probably aren't aware of this, but nine times out of ten, the couple didn't purchase the vases from the florist, so the florist takes those home at the end of the night. And the same was true in this situation. Even though I, as the planner, tried to explain to the drunk wedding party member that the couple couldn't take the vases home, I was met with so much opposition and insistence that the couple had paid for the flowers and were entitled to take everything. An easy solution was to have the couple pick up everything from the florist the next day since they couldn't physically take everything anyway. Then the florist could advise them of what they could and could not keep. *Problem solved!*

Hair and makeup are additional scenarios where members of the wedding party can show their entitlement. Whether it's a member of the wedding having the hairstylist or makeup artist do multiple looks because they're picky or opting out of hair and makeup altogether to work with their own hair and makeup team, the member of the wedding party feels entitled to this super high level of service. I get wanting to look your best, but if it's not your wedding day, then this is not about you. (For the record, I totally understand the scenario of someone choosing not to work with a hair and makeup team due to concerns that the hairstylist isn't equipped to work with their hair texture or the makeup artist doesn't have experience with their skin tone. An even better reason to make sure that you're hiring vendors that are capable and comfortable working with any and every individual!)

If at this point I've convinced you to think twice about having a wedding party, I do encourage you to give some thought to how you do want to involve your friends. It may not be something as significant as asking them to plan some of the traditional pre-wedding events; it might just be making sure that they are there with you on the wedding day for the getting ready part of the day. One of my clients opted for no wedding party and, after the fact, regretted it a bit. She found that the getting ready portion of her wedding day didn't quite have the energy and buzz that she had envisioned it having since she wasn't surrounded by her nearest and dearest that morning. That's not to say that if you opt to skip the wedding party, you can't invite all of your friends to get ready with you, but since she didn't have a wedding party, it wasn't as obvious who to invite to join her for that part of the day. And it wasn't something that she realized she missed until after the fact.

Been There, Done That

– by Jessica Jones*

name changed at author's request

My husband's best man at our wedding - we'll call him "Joe" - had been a friend since elementary school. They went to elementary, middle, and high school together. They grew up the same, but they ended up very differently. My husband is currently finishing his Doctoral degree in educational leadership, and Joe's life is very different. But none of that really matters when you're friends with somebody, so my husband and Joe are still friends. It was a natural thing to want him as his best man because they were considered best friends.

Our wedding had quite a lot to it. Not only did we have the full-blown wedding weekend, but we had a couple of events beforehand to get the wedding party together and let everybody have fun. We had a beach party that had a full-on Turkish beach theme where we had pillows and tents and food and games for the kids and all kinds of stuff like that for our wedding party.

We also had attire for our wedding party that was custom-made. The suit jackets were custom-made for the guys. The dresses were custom-made for the ladies. So, we had multiple times for Joe to be able to see how his life was different than my husband's current lifestyle. And I think that there was some jealousy there. When my husband was growing up with Joe, he was a late bloomer, and he was the cute guy, the funny guy, until probably freshman or sophomore year of college. Joe was always the cool guy. Always handsome. Always had the ladies. That kind of guy. So he had it all. And my husband wasn't really a threat to Joe.

But then, my husband grew up, and he got very handsome. He started living a lifestyle that was much different.

So now, here's our wedding. Husband has a different financial outlook, a better financial outlook. He's handsome. He's getting married. He's doing all of the things that I think Joe would've wanted to do if he had done it the "right way." And Joe saw all of this firsthand.

For the most part, everything seemed okay. There might have been little things here and there, little comments here and there from Joe. But on the wedding day, everything came to a head when Joe made our wedding late by an hour.

Joe, on the day of, claimed that he forgot his shoes, and whether he did it on purpose or not, he didn't have any shoes. But he didn't tell anyone until maybe 40 minutes or an hour or so before the wedding was set to start. He lived about 20, 30 minutes away from our venue. So, he demanded that my wedding planner put him in a black car - Uber Black - to send him to get his shoes and come back. Well, we live in a big city, so getting in a car and driving anywhere in traffic from downtown - anywhere - is a bit of a risk. But he did. And then, as he left, apparently, he told people, "Oh, they'll wait for me."

That was definitely not my goal - to have us wait for him - but I had no idea what was happening, and our planner made a poor decision not to just start without him. I was dressed and ready, waiting in the getting-ready room. I didn't really have a concept of time that day because I hired a wedding planner with five assistants, so I wasn't really worried about anything. That was the goal. That's why we paid the money for the wedding planner and the assistants. But she was kind of all over the place.

Eventually, I started feeling like, "I've been dressed for a long time; why is this taking so long?" I asked someone to pop out of the room and make sure the coast was clear. When it was, I popped my head out of the getting-ready room and got the attention of my wedding planner. But it just so happened that at that moment was when he was already walking in and he had his shoes. I didn't know at the time what was happening. I was like, "Okay, well, there's a little snag, but things seem to be okay." Then, no one was lined up. Nothing was going on. Nothing was in order. Because my wedding planner was too busy dealing with this one thing (Joe) that she didn't have any of her assistants doing anything else. So, we started the wedding an hour late.

The ceremony was gorgeous. It is still one of the happiest days of my life. And I had no idea really that we were even that late until the reception staff said something. As the reception was ending-- I didn't know it was ending, but it was ending - the people that worked there walked up to me, and they were so kind. Because we got married at a club that we were members of, we knew the staff, and they said, "Hey, we've already been here about an hour and 15 minutes longer than the agreement." Also, the boss was coming in to check to make sure that we were either cleaned up and out or on our way out. And I'm like, "Oh my gosh, I had no idea."

So, we basically had to bribe them. We had to bribe the staff to let us go over and not tell the boss. We ended up paying thousands of extra dollars in tips to the staff to avoid paying even more thousands of dollars for going over the venue time. And because of everything that had happened and the time being off - we didn't cut our cake the day of.

I think everyone's wedding feels a little rushed, but this really felt too rushed towards the end. I didn't know it at the time because I was like floating on cloud nine, but it was definitely rushed. Luckily, we had an after-party, so we still got to keep the party going.

As I look back, it was a shit show for timing and timeline. That's why your wedding planner really matters. Get a wedding planner who knows what they're doing. My planner was not a wedding planner. She was an event planner who didn't specialize in weddings. She's a wonderful human being, but looking back, I think it would've been better to have an actual wedding planner, or at least hire a wedding planner for the day of, that could really keep to the timeline, despite any kind of issues arising or people drama.

As far as my husband and his friend Joe are concerned, they're still friends. But ever since our wedding, they definitely kind of have grown apart a little bit. They talk, but they don't talk as much. And they'll hang out for events like birthdays and things like that, but they aren't as close, which is sad because I know that men have a hard time making and keeping friends. Actually, I think friendship, in general, can be difficult, regardless of your gender. But I do think that it was jealousy that fueled him to just say, "Oh, they'll wait on me." That, plus the ineptitude of my planner, created the perfect storm.

It's a sign of why you need to be very clear about what's happening with your wedding party and why you also need to have a planner that knows what to do when people do things that they don't even realize they're doing. I don't think that Joe intentionally made the wedding late. I don't think any of it was conscious. I think it was all subconscious. But it still happened, and it would have been nice to not have it happen.

Chapter 16:
Stay Weird, Wedding Guests

We love you, but can you like....not?

What You'll Learn:

- Guests misbehave at weddings. Finding humor in others' actions is a great way to know that their behavior isn't a reflection on you but on them.

- The root cause of a lot of this behavior is entitlement. Keep that in mind, and you'll have a better understanding of what's going on.

Picture the scene: A stunning wedding venue on a crisp fall day. A black-tie affair. A beautiful couple surrounded by all of their closest family and friends. Though by no definition a casual party, to keep the vibe a little less formal, this couple opted to have a floating supper reception where dinner is both passed and at stations and where there isn't assigned seating (or even a seat for every guest).

 **PRO TIP:** I have lots of feelings about floating supper receptions and often try to steer my couples away from them for a whole host of reasons – unless you have a mostly younger crowd, a lot of guests will be confused by not having a place to sit; it makes structuring the flow of the reception a little tricky; and it's challenging to feed guests enough food fast enough.

That last point was the exact downfall of this wedding. As food would come out of the kitchen, the same guests would stand right by the entrance and immediately take every item of food from the servers' trays. So, each server would make it a few steps into the space before having to return right back to the kitchen. In other words, food wasn't making it to most of the crowd. At this point, guests started getting grumpy, harassing me about why there wasn't more food, and then several guests walked into the kitchen and took food from the counters where it was waiting to be plated. It got so bad that I had to stand at the entrance to the kitchen to physically block guests from entering.

Now, if you were at a restaurant and really hungry and the food wasn't coming out quickly enough, would you ever dream of getting up, walking into the kitchen, and just taking food off of a counter? *Absolutely not!* And yet, when it comes to weddings, people think this is acceptable behavior.

Admittedly, this might be my favorite chapter because this is where all the unbelievable wedding stories have their home. People behaving badly is just par for the course when it comes to weddings (both prior to the wedding and at the wedding itself), and for some reason, weddings embolden people to do things that they would never do outside of this setting.

Here are just a few of the wild stories I've heard and seen first-hand:

- A friend of mine in catering once told me about one of her weddings where someone cut a piece of cake for themselves before the couple had done the official cake cutting. You might think that this was a kid who did this, someone who didn't know better. But no, it was the adult aunt of one of the people getting married who was just "hungry" and didn't feel like waiting until later for cake. *Seriously?*

- A DJ I work with frequently regaled me with the tale of a groom's sister at one of his weddings who was getting alcoholic drinks for her underage sons from the bar. Even after being confronted by one of the bartenders about how that was ILLEGAL, the behavior continued. She started putting vodka in water bottles for her boys so that people couldn't tell what they were drinking. The joke was on her because she ended up spending most of the reception tending to her kids, who were throwing up in the bathroom after drinking too much. *Karma, baby.*

• A couple I know who eloped at City Hall later had a celebratory weekend with their immediate family and closest friends only. Two members of one partner's immediate family declined the invite because it wasn't a "real" wedding. Would you ever decline an invite for someone's birthday party under the reasoning that the party wasn't on the person's actual birthday? Why do weddings make people behave this way?

• I'll never forget my client, who texted me a photo of one of the RSVP cards she received back. It was from a couple that was friends with the groom's parents. The couple themselves couldn't go, but in place of their names, they wrote in the name of their adult daughter, who, for the record, the couple had never even met, nor was she even invited. That's not how this works, people!

Seating Shenanigans

When it comes to seating assignments for a wedding, I always tell my couples that you must assign guests to a specific table because people need some level of direction—otherwise, it's like a middle school cafeteria. However, you don't need to assign guests a specific seat.

I say that for a few reasons:

• Selfishly, it's a pain in the ass for me to have to put out individual place cards for 150+ guests.

• While guests appreciate being assigned to a specific table, they generally don't want to be told what seat they must sit in.

• It's *so much work* for the couple to assign every guest to an individual seat, and I'd rather have them not stress about it and spend their time more wisely.

• Your guests are going to move their place cards around anyway. I've had guests move place cards around while I was literally standing right next to them. One woman looked up and realized I had seen what she did and told me that she needed to move her father to another seat. "Trust me, it's the best thing for everyone," she said. *Uh-huh.*

When place cards are involved, I triple-check the seating arrangements. I first put all the cards in their places according to the seating chart I've been given. Then once all the cards are out, I go back through and check everything against the chart. And then, just before guests enter for dinner, I go through and check everything a third time. Why so thorough? Because I know that if anyone is not where they are supposed to be, I'm going to inevitably get a question from the couple about why so and so isn't sitting in their assigned seat.

At a recent wedding, I was on my third round of place card checks just before dinner when I noticed that a few cards were out of order at one table. A couple was standing nearby, and I asked them if they had moved the cards around. They said no but did admit that those were their names on the cards. I put everything back in order, just annoyed that someone had come in and changed things up. This couple leaves, and I go over to chat with the DJ, joking about why people can't just sit where they are supposed to. And he goes, "Yeah, that couple that just left totally moved around their cards." Are you kidding me? They lied right to my face. *At least if you're going to break the rules, have the courage to own up to it.*

A Toast to... *Toasts*

Toasts are also ripe for inappropriate behavior. What is it that makes people think getting up in front of a room full of strangers and sharing embarrassing stories or giving sexist advice is acceptable? Why on earth would a best person think that people would want to hear the retelling of a story about the couple and their friends sharing a villa on vacation and him being able to hear the couple having sex next door? Also, if I had a dollar for every time a parent told a hetero couple that "a happy wife makes for a happy life" or "the woman is always right," I'd be a millionaire at this point. Another common offender is the family member or friend who includes a line in the toast about how they can't wait for the couple to start having kids or how they hope the couple will change their minds about not wanting to have kids. Come on; it's not even right to say that kind of thing in private, much less in front of a crowd at someone's wedding.

One woman who shared her wedding experience with me for the book summed this concept up pretty nicely: "I was surprised by how others will try to make it about them or how the negative aspects of their personality will really come through."

Sometimes, you just have to laugh to keep from crying. And when it comes to guests' behavior, that's probably the best advice I can give you.

When Entitlement Comes into Play

In 2016, the American Psychological Association published an article by Julie J. Exline and Joshua B. Grubbs titled "Trait Entitlement: A Cognitive-Personality Source of Vulnerability to Psychological Distress." As a wedding planner, I find a LOT of entitlement when it comes to weddings and often wonder where it comes from.

Exline and Grubbs define psychological entitlement as "a personality trait characterized by pervasive feelings of deservingness, specialness, and exaggerated expectations." The accompanying idea to that definition is that an entitled individual didn't do anything to earn the benefits (the goods, services, or special treatment) that they feel entitled to. Apply that definition in the context of a wedding, and some of the behavior you'll see starts to make a lot more sense.

Think back to the story I shared at the start of this chapter about the hungry guests who walked into the catering kitchen and just started grabbing food. Like I said, they would never do something like that at a restaurant, but being a guest at a wedding gave them a sense of entitlement – that they were special as a result of having been invited, the rules didn't apply to them, and they deserved food at the exact moment they wanted it. *How dare someone make them wait to be served?*

That same entitled mindset comes into play when it comes to the ridiculousness that I've seen with seating assignments, also mentioned above. Those guests have an inflated sense of their importance at the wedding and feel like the couple's decision on their seating assignment doesn't matter. *How dare the couple tell them where to sit?*

After setting the stage for what entitlement is, Exline and Grubbs go on to explain some of the emotions that can manifest when someone feels entitled. You see, if someone feels entitled or special or deserving, but they haven't actually done anything to earn that status, then the world isn't going to treat that person the way that person thinks they should be treated. And when someone doesn't get the goods, services, or special treatment that they think they deserve, what do you think is going to happen? Obviously, that person is going to get angry.

Tell a wedding guest that they can't do something ("No, you can't take shots at the bar" or "No, the DJ can't play one more song"), and you'll see their mood totally shift. It's not uncommon to get a snippy, "I'm going to go talk to the couple about this," when not catering to someone's every whim. You also have to keep in mind that feelings of entitlement and the potentially resulting anger get exacerbated by alcohol and tiredness. I know I'm probably not my best self at 1 a.m. if I've been up all day and drinking for the last five hours.

Feelings of entitlement are also enhanced when spending money. Whether it's the couple, a family member, or friend who is contributing financially to the wedding, that person is going to feel entitled to *more* because they are paying the bill. In a way, you can't fault someone for feeling like that. Of course, if you're spending a lot of money to have this wedding, you're going to feel entitled (rightfully or wrongly) to certain things in return. Yes, there's a level of service that you should be receiving from your venue and vendors that's commensurate with the price tag, but to expect those people to cater to your every desire and every whim is probably outside the scope of your contract.

And if you're someone getting married and you're reading this and feeling appalled by people's behavior, you, my friend, are not immune. As the person getting married, feeling an inflated sense of self is easier to slip into than you might think, especially because of the stress and anxiety you're feeling during the planning process. In any other context, when you're stressed out, think about how snippy you can get when things don't go your way. Now imagine that coupled with the pressure of planning a wedding, and you can see how easy it is to go down that path. It's also helpful to remember that acting on feelings of entitlement often leads to interpersonal conflict, so if maintaining positive relationships with those around you during the wedding planning process is a priority, then it's going to be important to stay mindful about exhibiting entitled behavior.

"Look, wedding planning is not for everyone and even as a wedding planner who loves her job, I get that. Feeling relief that the wedding is over, that your lives can go back to business as usual, and that you can finally talk about something else is a perfectly fine place to be. Planning a wedding is stressful – there is no getting around that fact – and not everyone enjoys the process. So, to have a phenomenal wedding day experience but still not want to put yourself through that again is a natural reaction."

– Leah Weinberg

A Parting Word on Post-Wedding Feelings

The Moment It's Over

Picture this: You spend "x" number of months planning this significant life event. There is so much anticipation and excitement leading up to the wedding day. You get to the day itself and find yourself enveloped in so much love, happiness, and pure joy with your family and friends. The day is hands down amazing, and you simply don't want it to end. You look over at your partner and say, "Let's do this every weekend!" The time and money and stress were all worth it, and you would do it again in a heartbeat if you could.

As I've said many times, while your wedding day is not the most important day of your life, it *is* a rare experience for people. How often in a lifetime do you get to gather *all* of your favorite people on the planet in one room to celebrate a milestone moment? Not often. So, once you've experienced it, it might be something you want to do again and again.

On the other hand, you might have had an incredible wedding day and didn't want it to end, but there's no chance in hell that you would *ever* want to do it again. That reaction is totally valid as well!

Look, wedding planning is not for everyone, and even as a wedding planner who loves her job, I get that. Feeling relief that the wedding is over, that your lives can go back to business as usual, and that you can finally talk about something else is a perfectly fine place to be. Planning a wedding is stressful – there is no getting around that fact – and not everyone enjoys the process. So, to have a phenomenal wedding day experience but still not want to put yourself through that again is a natural reaction.

If this book is any indication, I am clearly very interested in understanding the underlying causes of the emotions and behavior that come with weddings. Quite possibly, the aspect of all this that fascinates me the most is how couples view their wedding *after the fact*. I'll be the first to admit that I am incredibly picky, have high expectations of people, and am very detail-oriented. But when it came to my own wedding day, I was definitely *not* looking for something to be wrong or out of place, nor did I look back on the day trying to find something that hadn't gone according to plan. In fact, I remember being on our honeymoon, making sure that I visualized and relived the day so that I could capture in my memory all the amazing moments rather than having it all be a blur. *That exercise was rooted in positivity, and as you look back, I want you to share in that positive mindset too.*

Based on my own experience, as someone who is, again, very particular, the fact that I didn't look back and nitpick my day makes me wonder why on earth anyone else would, but it happens. Probably more than you think. So, let's look at some of the post-wedding feelings that might arise and how you can proactively keep them from creeping into your life.

Why Setting Realistic Expectations Is Important for How You Feel Afterwards

I wrote early on about dispelling the notion that your wedding will be the best day of your life. I tackled that topic at the beginning because setting realistic expectations for your wedding day underlies everything else that I talk about in this book, and it impacts every part of the wedding planning process – the before, during, *and* after.

Christy Matthews and Michelle Martinez, hosts of The Big Wedding Planning Podcast, like to remind their listeners that you're on this journey with your partner of meeting, dating, falling in love, getting engaged, then at the end of the day you're going to be married. There just happens to be a giant party along the way. Your primary focus *should* be on the whole process and the adventure that awaits once you're married – it should *not* be on the party that happens somewhere in the middle.

To clarify, being excited about your wedding celebration is to be expected (and encouraged!), but setting high expectations for what the day is going to be like and feel like puts you at risk of feeling let down afterward or for scrutinizing it to find out what went wrong. That's why we have to adjust those expectations on the front end. Going back to the wisdom from Jesse Kahn, psychotherapist and sex therapist from The Gender & Sexuality Therapy Center, you and your partner should discuss in advance what your wedding day celebration means to the two of you, what you expect out of it, and how you want to feel on your wedding day. Verbalizing (or putting on paper) those wants and needs will help you stay grounded along the way and relieve the pressure of your wedding day having to be something bigger, better, and more important than what you really desire (or having to be what society tells you it's supposed to be).

The other thing to keep in mind when setting realistic expectations about your wedding is to make sure you view it in the context of your entire relationship. While it's likely going to be a great day, it is still just *one day* out of many in your time together.

Weddings Are Kind of Like a Group Project

Another component of the wedding planning process that makes it unique and makes couples susceptible to an emotional letdown afterward is that wedding planning is likely the first major "project" that you and your partner have worked on together so closely. Let's be real; planning a wedding *can* get all-consuming if you let it. You and your partner might find yourselves talking about it every time you have some time together, which is why you'll see a lot of planning how-to books tell you to schedule wedding planning time with your partner once or twice a week. *Draw those boundaries!*

If you find yourselves out on a rare date night during the week, talk about what's going on at work or with your families rather than what you want as a first dance song. Or talk about what movies are coming out that you're excited about rather than what cake flavors you like. It's critical to create space between your relationship and the wedding planning process so that your relationship doesn't just become about planning a wedding. If wedding planning is all you and your partner are connecting on for however many months (or years) leading up to your wedding, once the wedding is over, you might find yourselves asking, "What's next?" or "How do we spend time together now?" You might feel a little out of sorts now that you no longer have the thing that you were bonding over for a good amount of time.

So, if you end up not being good about drawing boundaries while planning your wedding (I'll admit that I certainly wasn't!), you'll need to be mindful and proactive post-wedding about connecting with your partner in conversation and in doing activities together.

The silver lining in all of this is that however pleasant (or unpleasant) you and your partner find the wedding planning process, you're going to be building some serious communication, decision making, and teamwork skills for the future. A thoughtful approach to wedding planning with your partner can set you up for serious success when it comes to navigating future events, like moving, buying a home, changing careers, starting a business, or making additions to the family (whether they be fur or human children).

How You Look Back

I mentioned that I took time to intentionally reflect on my wedding day to cement the day in my memory. And even though the day did go by so fast, I wanted to be able to remember the moments big and small, like one of my best friends from high school making sure that I got a few extra bites of cake after the cake cutting. Having a short but sweet conversation with a friend who flew all the way from New York with her husband to be there for my wedding. And dancing to "Footloose" with all my favorite people on the dance floor at the end of the night.

For my husband and me, it was a great day, and I wanted to look back with only a positive lens. I didn't want to nitpick every moment to identify what went wrong. That's not what I wanted to remember. And I implore you to do the same. Try not to go back over your wedding day with a fine-tooth comb and say things like, "This person's speech was too long," or "They didn't say the things that I had hoped they would say," or "So and so didn't show up at the last minute" (pro tip: that happens *all* the time so you might as well prepare for it), or "My parents got into a fight." None of that. Don't go back moment by moment to try to figure out what went wrong. Honestly, just try to have rose-colored glasses when you're looking back at your wedding day.

If everything was fantastic, for the most part, don't go back and look for something wrong. That's not going to serve you at all. It's better to have this amazing, glowing feeling about your wedding rather than thinking about every little thing that happened and finding something that went sideways. That intense focus on negative scrutiny is just going to weigh you down, and letting go of any unnecessary negative feelings will be freeing.

A great way to mindfully reflect on your wedding day and to help you remember and capture details is to journal about the day shortly thereafter. If you've got the time and want a rather detailed account, think through the entire day and write about it from start to finish. Or, if that sounds too daunting and time-consuming (remember, this should be an enjoyable experience and not feel like homework), think back to your favorite moments from the day and write about those. Include details on what happened, but don't forget to also write about your emotions and how those moments made you *feel*. With things fresh in your mind, you'll be able to create an incredible account of your wedding day to have for the future, and by intentionally focusing on the positive, you can cement in your mind the happiest moments from your wedding.

All of that being said, while I encourage you, post-wedding, to not focus on anything negative from your wedding day, some couples do, and you might feel the need to as well. If you do find yourself in that position, then get curious about those feelings, as Jesse Kahn suggests.

Ask yourself *why* you're looking back on the wedding day the way you are. Is it because something significant went wrong? Is it because a situation happened that caused you emotional pain? Is it because there's something deeper going on and you don't feel entitled to the happiness of that day? Kahn confirms your day doesn't have to be wonderful and that you might have to focus on something painful from the day in order to process it. But do be mindful of the *why* behind this scrutiny and be introspective about your approach.

I hate to sound like a broken record here, but how you look back also has to do with the expectations you had for the wedding going into the event.

Reality can indeed be the great equalizer. That's why it's so important to take the pressure off your wedding day and get on the same page with your partner as to how you want the day to both look and feel. If you're hoping for a super romantic day straight out of a fairy tale while your partner is looking forward to an epic dance party—you both might be in for a surprise. Setting expectations early on can lead to much better memories.

While my wish for you is nothing but rosy memories of your wedding day, if there is something you need to address or process, be mindful of why and how you go about doing that.

The Most Important Mindset

Mmmmmmm, as a planner, I *love* a couple with a go-with-the-flow mindset. While I wouldn't call it a *cure* for post-wedding blues, it's one way to give yourself a head start to a positive mental state. While I try to do everything in my power to troubleshoot each couple's wedding day, predict what *could* go wrong, and then take steps to make sure it doesn't, there is always a possibility something won't go according to plan. (Though that one thing is probably going to be small and something the couple never expected!)

One of my clients dropped something on her toe just before the rehearsal dinner and, while it was bruised and possibly broken, she put some tape on it, showed up to the wedding with a smile, and chalked it up to that being the one thing that would go wrong at her wedding. (I'm happy to report nothing else went awry — that I know of! — on the wedding day). One of my grooms split his lip open playing basketball the day before the wedding and had to go to the emergency room for stitches. And while he couldn't make the biggest smile for pictures, the couple were total troopers and didn't let that negatively impact their day in the slightest.

It's all about having a positive mindset and a willingness to be flexible. I like to tell my clients that once you get to the point in the wedding week where family and friends start to arrive, everything is just going to keep rolling from there. Once we're at the wedding day, we've done all we can to prepare and anticipate anything going astray, so if something happens, there's frankly not a lot we can do to fix it in most cases, so you're just going to have to roll with it, go with the flow, and try not to let it bother you.

One of my favorite stories is from one of my couples who had a close friend officiate their ceremony. Their friend was *so* excited to be officiating, and as a generally gregarious and outgoing person, he had no nerves at all in taking on this role. His nerves were, in fact, so non-existent that he decided to "wing it" for the ceremony rather than reading from the script he had prepared.

PRO TIP: To be clear, this is *not* something I recommend for any officiant, no matter how confident they are in their officiating abilities. Not even the pros try to do it without a script or their notes in front of them.

All was well and good until we got to the end of the ceremony; he pronounced my couple husband and wife, they kissed, guests cheered, and then the couple and the officiant realized that he had *skipped* the exchange of rings. Total facepalm moment. But they annexed the ring exchange to the end of the ceremony, he repronounced them husband and wife, they kissed, guests cheered, and everyone recessed back down the aisle. What was, let's be honest, a pretty big gaffe when it comes to a wedding ceremony turned into a memorable comedic experience. While the couple could have been upset with their officiant, they just went with it and now have a hilarious story to tell rather than letting it ruin their day.

Also, when it comes to things not going according to plan, chances are that no one is going to notice. Early in my career, I had a client who was majorly disappointed in her flowers. While she had been envisioning a color palette of pinks, oranges, and yellows, the florist delivered a bouquet and centerpieces that were predominantly pink. Now don't get me wrong, the flowers were absolutely gorgeous with coral charm peonies aplenty, but my client knew that they weren't right and weren't what she wanted. However, no one else at the wedding had any clue that the flowers were anything other than what the couple ordered. She kept bringing up her disappointment with the flowers, and I kept reassuring her that the flowers were stunning and that no one would know there was anything wrong. Eventually, she said, "I just have to let this go, don't I?" and I politely told her that yes, she was just going to have to go with at that point because it wasn't like we had time for the florist to go back to the flower market and redo everything.

So, what's the lesson here? Go with the flow because sometimes it is what it is, and we just don't have the time or the ability to change it.

Buyer's Remorse

Unless you and your partner have bought a home before (together or separately), the amount of money you're going to spend on a wedding is probably the most money you've ever spent on a single thing ever. I would imagine you've never spent over $1,000 on a cake before or paid thousands of dollars to have your photo taken or ever dreamed that you'd be contemplating spending $10,000+ on flowers that go on dinner tables.

With spending that much money comes pretty high expectations for what you're going to get in return. (See, it all comes back to those pesky expectations.) It's natural to equate a price tag with a certain level of quality or with a sense of how you're going to feel, but those expectations still need to be managed. Otherwise, you're going to find yourself with a big ole case of buyer's remorse after the wedding is over.

To be proactive about addressing buyer's remorse, you've got to start tackling it at the beginning. Creating a realistic budget is vital because it establishes what you and your partner (and sometimes families) are comfortable spending *before* you get wrapped up in the emotions and excitement of wedding planning. That budget is going to reflect amounts that you agreed to spend while you were in a grounded mindset and not once you're caught up in the allure of a disco ball installation over your dance floor.

I've said it before, but talking about money is always really uncomfortable, particularly if you're getting money from other sources and not funding the wedding yourselves. Saying to your parents flat out, "How much money are you giving me for this wedding?" is, for most people, a really uncomfortable question to ask. But you have to do it. You need to know at the beginning how much you have to spend and how much everyone is *comfortable* spending.

If it helps you to manage your expectations or ease some guilt in spending so much money on a single event, you also have the option of *not* spending every penny that you've budgeted for the wedding. As I mentioned previously, I've worked with a lot of couples who have said to me, "We have this much to spend, but we'd actually prefer to keep it under that budget and not spend that full amount." They're making that conscious choice to not feel super exorbitant or wasteful with the money they have or that they've been given.

Knowing what your budget is and being very mindful of trying to stick to that budget is going to help you not feel so bad post-wedding about how much money you spent. That's not to say you won't ever question your decisions. Even I – someone who loved every minute of her wedding— will look back sometimes on how much money we spent and wish that I had a little bit of that money in savings right now. Thoughts like that are going to happen, but if you've been conscious of your mindset from the start – from your expectations to agreeing on a comfort level with your spending – you'll have an advantage post-wedding in not getting consumed by those feelings.

Another thing to avoid in order to prevent buyer's remorse is making decisions that are driven by the excitement of the day approaching or that mindset of, "What's another 'x' number of dollars at this point?" Check yourself when it comes to making emotional spending decisions as you get closer to the wedding because those are the ones you are most likely to regret. You might panic three weeks before the wedding, fearing that the venue will feel too sparse, so you give the florist a few extra thousand dollars to go super lush with the arrangements. Then you get to the wedding day and realize it totally wasn't necessary. That's the kind of last-minute decision I want you to be conscious of.

Working with a planner is also going to help you avoid these on-the-spot reactions that involve spending more money. I consider it part of my job to be a gut check for my couples when it comes to their spending. I will give my honest opinion when couples ask whether it's worth a last-minute upgrade to their bar package for top-shelf liquor (after a cocktail or two, can anyone *really* tell the difference between brands?) or a decision to order a dozen pizzas for a late-night snack (generally not too cost-prohibitive and who doesn't love late-night pizza?!).

One of my couples came to me a few weeks out from their wedding saying they had some extra money to put towards the wedding. My first question was, "Are you sure you want to spend more money on the wedding?" and when they said yes, my next step was to help them figure out how best to spend it. Initially, the couple had wanted to spend about $2,000 to have a barista come in after dinner to serve espresso drinks during dessert. But then the bride (one of my most color-loving clients to date) told me that she had a dream about the disco ball over their dance floor having a flower crown. Talk about a sign! Having the florist do an installation around the disco ball would not only be less expensive, but I knew it would bring her so much joy, so I weighed in and told the couple that that was where I felt their money would be best spent. They agreed, and I am happy to report that the disco ball floral installation was a stunner!

When spending money on a wedding, in most cases, you're going to get what you paid for. The vendor did their job, gave you what you asked for, and if it didn't match exactly what you had in your mind or didn't give you a sensation of total excitement, that's probably coming from something internal on your end as opposed to any shortfall in the service that was provided. But what happens when it's clear that a vendor *has* screwed up and it has an impact on your day? When the feeling goes from a small case of buyer's remorse to "we actually didn't get what we paid for."

Vendor Mistakes

I pride myself on the fact that 19 times out of 20, when a vendor has a misstep at a wedding, my clients never know about it. *But,* when something does happen that's a little more public, depending on the impact it has, there may have to be some post-wedding conversations with the couple on how to address it. On a few occasions, a band or DJ has missed a cue or played the wrong song at the wrong time, which is admittedly a pretty basic (though significant) mistake for a seasoned pro, but at the end of the day, what impact did that have? Did it ruin the day? And in the case of the wrong song being played, did anyone other than the couple and me even know? For the record, sometimes the couple is so wrapped up in the moment that even *they* don't notice. If it's a slip-up like that, I generally don't encourage the couple to go to the vendor afterward to discuss it.

However, know that your planner is for sure going to address the situation and not let something like that slide; they are going to advocate for you. For the band that failed to cue the recording of the processional song, I went up to them right after and asked, "What just happened?" But for the couple, what's that song worth? How can you put a price on something like that when your day was overall phenomenal and there was that one hiccup?

But, when you *have* had a negative experience with a vendor that resulted in you not getting what you paid for or a moment that had a real impact on your day, I suggest following these three steps:

Step One: Start with a conversation. A friend shared a story with me about a client of hers who was unhappy with the cake at her bridal shower. The cake itself was prepared by a very reputable baker and looked gorgeous, so of course, many photos were taken of the cake at the shower. It was served and totally devoured. After the shower, my friend's client came to her and stated she wanted a full refund of the cake because it didn't have enough almond flavor. At that point, the cake was gone, so no refund could be given. What the client could do was share (with grace) how the cake lacked the flavor she desired, and the baker may have offered to do something special or fix the issue another way, furthering the relationship.

Step Two: If the situation warrants it, ask for a refund (but only of what's truly owed). For one of my clients, the dress shop gave her the wrong veil, which unfortunately she didn't notice until she opened the box to put on the veil on the day of the wedding. If something like that occurs, you should go back to the store and ask for a refund. But in terms of demanding money beyond the refund, what purpose does that serve? What does that get you? The veil the bride received instead was still gorgeous and wearable, and no one else knew it wasn't the right veil. So, it's not like it would make sense to ask for more money for any kind of emotional distress. It's one thing to want to make the situation right, and it's another to be punitive.

Step Three: Leave a negative review. Now, I'm going to let you in on a little secret (or maybe a not-so-secret). Small business owners have nightmares about receiving bad reviews online. We could have 50 amazing 5-star reviews from clients who love and adore us, but that one negative (or even less than 5-star) review haunts us forever. It's partly because we will forever be asked about that one review by prospective clients (and that's if the review doesn't turn them off from contacting us in the first place), but it's also because most of us in the wedding industry are perfectionists and our number one goal is to make our clients infinitely happy. So, when we fail to do that, it's soul-crushing.

I am admittedly 100% biased when I say this, but please consider leaving a negative review or sharing negative feedback online as a last resort. You should first have a conversation with the vendor whose performance you were unhappy with and then request a refund should the situation warrant it. But if the vendor accepts your feedback and gives you the refund you ask for, leaving a negative review after that is just malicious. Like if the dress shop refused to refund the veil my client paid for and didn't receive (after multiple attempts to calmly speak with them about it), then by all means, go to town with your negative reviews. But if you get what you wanted from the vendor, bashing them publicly is totally unnecessary. Believe me; a good vendor is going to feel bad enough for the mistake without you dragging their name through the mud online.

Now What?

If your wedding has come and gone and you find yourself in your feelings a bit, know that it's not uncommon to feel that way, but also don't marinate in those feelings for too long. If the wedding wasn't what you expected, come to terms with those emotions and try to move forward. At the end of the day, you still got married! If you and your partner are at a loss for things to talk about and how to spend time together now that the wedding is over, plan some activities to help the two of you connect, like dining out at your favorite restaurant, going for a stroll through your neighborhood, or exploring a local museum. If you are starting to regret how much money you spent, remind yourself that you thoughtfully spent that money but also that what's done is done, you're married, and you got what you paid for. And if you find yourself in the unfortunate position of having a vendor who didn't do their job, I encourage you to handle the situation with dignity and grace but still advocate for yourself.

It's been almost a decade since my own wedding, and I still look back on that day with immense joy and the desire to do it all again. People often ask if there's anything I would do differently, and honestly, there isn't. Well, except for the chairs. If I could do it all over again, I would *definitely* pay to upgrade the chairs. Chairs aside, my wedding day was an overwhelming success!

For me, that day was also more significant than I ever knew at the time because it kicked off another roller coaster ride for me – that of entrepreneurship. Similarly, what comes next for you and your partner will be filled with even more ups and downs than your wedding planning process. And while I know this book doesn't specifically address everything that's yet to come, I hope that some of the skills and practices contained within these pages will stick with you for the journey ahead.

Afterword

I LOVE theme parks. At the start of 2020, I spent an entire week at Disney World with a dear friend going on every ride imaginable, taking cheesy photos with all the characters, and eating all the Mickey-shaped sweets we could get our hands on. The last day we were there, we managed to set foot in all four parks in a single day – *maybe one of my proudest achievements.*

Part of my love of theme parks has to do with my love for roller coasters. I'm not afraid of heights, I'm up for trying any coaster at least once, and I'd say my favorites are ones where you can't see what's coming next, like Space Mountain – the *best* ride at Disney World. I'll be in line, super excited to board, my adrenaline pumping. And then, as soon as I'm seated and the cars start slowing moving up that first hill, I always experience the same emotions.

I start freaking out, wondering what on earth I've done. Most often, I'm yelling expletives at the person sitting beside me or silently mouthing them if I'm next to a stranger. That slow climb always feels like an eternity, and then, once I'm over the first hump, the entire ride is all sheer terror and utter glee.

Sound familiar? That's what wedding planning can be like. Think about it: you've found a partner that you love and with whom you want to spend the rest of your life. Assuming that marriage is what the two of you ultimately want, you find yourself super excited at the prospect of getting engaged and can't wait to plan a celebration that represents the two of you. There is so much anticipation of the engagement, and you can sometimes barely contain your excitement. It's like the feeling of waiting in line to ride the roller coaster.

Then, whether one partner proposes to the other, both of you propose to each other, or you just decide to get married without much fanfare, you're engaged, and you board the roller coaster. Once it's official, you and your partner start thinking about dates and venues and color palettes and a guest list, and you quickly say to yourself, "What the f*ck have we gotten ourselves into?" That's the slow climb up the first hill on the roller coaster. *The wedding roller coaster.*

My hope is that this book has made you feel better about climbing that first hill and will be a guide through all the ups and downs, twists and turns, and loop-de-loops that await you on this ride. My wish for you is that you now have the tools for turning inwards to ask yourself the tough questions, to have deep and productive conversations with your partner, and to navigate your relationships with all the family and friends who are involved (no matter how intimately or not) in your wedding planning process.

It's not going to be all sunshine and rainbows ahead, but just know that I'm along on this ride with you, here to remind you that you'll get through this, and you can do it without sacrificing important relationships along the way. Just remember that there are so many adventures and new rides ahead once this one is over. Maybe that'll be the topic of my next book. Until then, I want to know: Was this helpful? Do you have more questions? Is there an experience you've had while wedding planning that I missed? I welcome any questions and feedback you may have! Feel free to send those to hello@colorpopevents.com.

And if you enjoyed what you read, I would be honored if you could leave me a review on Amazon!

Acknowledgments

This book would not have been possible without the help and support of so many people. I've done my best to list them below, and if there's anyone I missed, please know that I adore and appreciate you!

Thank you to Alexis Buryk, Meghan Ely, Sarah Kelman, Jen McDowell, Christie Osborne, and Crystal Whiteaker for reading early drafts of this book, providing invaluable feedback, and giving me the words of encouragement that I didn't know I needed. I am so grateful to all of you!

Thank you to Justin McCallum for answering a ton of random questions, sharing his wisdom, and providing such helpful feedback for the book.

Thank you to Renée Dalo for being my accountability buddy and sending encouraging text messages.

Thank you to Kirsten Palladino for going above and beyond to support me and share her own experience as a published author.

Thank you to the people responsible for an amazing launch who help me with marketing, promotion, and content: Dani Boglivi-Fiori (my custom cookie queen), Meghan Ely and the whole team at OFD Consulting (my PR mavens), Aleya Harris (my StoryBrand expert and website content genius), Dami Okuboyejo (my gifting queen), Christie Osborne (my social media ads expert and Colorful Conversations producer), and Shannon Vonderach (my email marketing guru, website developer, and amazing human).

Thank you to Kate-Madonna (Hindes) Sieger, my editor and coach, to whom I owe the world. And thank you to Joe Selness, who proofread the crap out of this book, and to Gregory Rohm, who gave me the cover and book design I dreamed of.

Thank you to my friends and experts who shared their expertise that made this book better than I ever imagined: Trae Bodge, Shirin Eskandani, Callie Exas, Jesse Kahn, Petronella Lugemwa, and Meera Mohan-Graham.

Thank you to all of the individuals who contributed their personal stories for the Been There, Done That sections: Trae Bodge, Shirin Eskandani, Callie Exas, Cara Kaufman, Pooja Kothari, Justin McCallum, Jacob Passy, Liz Rosado, and two other individuals who preferred to contribute anonymously.

I know I've already mentioned her (twice!), but I owe a lot to Christie Osborne of Mountainside Media when it comes to this book. Christie is the person who has known about the book from almost the very beginning. She and I worked together on a content marketing strategy, and as part of that work, Christie did a ton of research on what wedding books were already out there and where my book would fit in the marketplace. She identified a gap for a book that encourages couples to make the wedding their own but not to lose sight of maintaining healthy relationships in the process. That's obviously a very simplified version of what she came up with, but the insight she provided me on the marketplace and the clarity she helped me get on the purpose of my book has been my guiding star for the few years that this has been in the works. The work she has done (and continues to do) with me has helped me stay on a very clear path with this project and make sure that I never lose sight of what this book is really all about.

Thank you to my crew at home for making this book possible and being the best #quaranteam a woman could ask for: Marc, Spike, and Bunsen. I love you all to the moon and back!

And last but certainly not least, thank you to all of my clients whose experiences gave me the insight and opportunity to write this book. Without you all, none of this would have been possible!

Sources

Chapter 1: Start with the Heart Work and Set Expectations

Interview with Jesse Kahn, LCSW-R, CST, an NYC-based psychotherapist and sex therapist and the Founder and Director at The Gender & Sexuality Therapy Center (https://gstherapycenter.com/)

Interview with Shirin Eskandani, a mindset and mindfulness coach and the founder of Whole Hearted Coaching (https://www.wholehearted-coaching.com/)

Psychology for Dummies, by Adam Cash, PsyD (Hoboken: John Wiley & Sons, Inc., 2013)

www.psychologytoday.com

Chapter 2: The Big, Uncomfortable Talks

Interview with Trae Bodge, a lifestyle journalist and TV commentator who specializes in smart shopping (https://truetrae.com/)

Chapter 5: Crafting a Wedding that Feels Like the Two of You

Interview with Meera Mohan-Graham, a wedding planning advocate and coach (https://meeragraham.com/)

Interview with Petronella Lugemwa, an NYC-based wedding photographer (https://bypetronella.com/)

Chapter 7: Your Communication Toolkit

Psychology for Dummies, by Adam Cash, PsyD (Hoboken: John Wiley & Sons, Inc., 2013)

Interview with Jesse Kahn, LCSW-R, CST, an NYC-based psychotherapist and sex therapist and the Founder and Director at The Gender & Sexuality Therapy Center (https://gstherapycenter.com/)

Chapter 8: Fixating on "Normal" and Other Unhelpful Lines of Thinking

Interview with Jesse Kahn, LCSW-R, CST, an NYC-based psychotherapist and sex therapist and the Founder and Director at The Gender & Sexuality Therapy Center (https://gstherapycenter.com/)

Psychology for Dummies, by Adam Cash, PsyD (Hoboken: John Wiley & Sons, Inc., 2013)

www.psychologytools.org

Chapter 9: Wedding Planning Can Be Stressful

Psychology for Dummies, by Adam Cash, PsyD (Hoboken: John Wiley & Sons, Inc., 2013)

Interview with Callie Exas, MPH, MS, RDN, and women's health, nutrition, and fitness expert (https://callieexas.com/)

Chapter 10: A Roller Coaster of Emotions

Psychology for Dummies, by Adam Cash, PsyD (Hoboken: John Wiley & Sons, Inc., 2013)

On Death and Dying by Elisabeth Kübler-Ross (New York: Scribner, 1969)

Interview with Meera Mohan-Graham, a wedding planning advocate and coach (https://meeragraham.com/)

Chapter 12: What It's Really About and What to Do About It

Interview with Jesse Kahn, LCSW-R, CST, an NYC-based psychotherapist and sex therapist and the Founder and Director at The Gender & Sexuality Therapy Center (https://gstherapycenter.com/)

Psychology for Dummies, by Adam Cash, PsyD (Hoboken: John Wiley & Sons, Inc., 2013)

Psych 101: Psychology Facts, Basics, Statistics, Tests, and More!, by Paul Kleinman (Avon: Adams Media, 2012)

Chapter 13: It's a Family Affair

Psychology for Dummies, by Adam Cash, PsyD (Hoboken: John Wiley & Sons, Inc., 2013)

Chapter 14: The Id, the Ego, and the Superego Walk into a Bar....

Psych 101: Psychology Facts, Basics, Statistics, Tests, and More!, by Paul Kleinman (Avon: Adams Media, 2012)

Disarming the Narcissist: Surviving and Thriving with the Self-Absorbed by Wendy Behary (Oakland: New Harbinger Publications, 2013)

Chapter 15: Your Wedding Party

https://www.nytimes.com/2019/02/06/fashion/weddings/when-weddings-ruin-friendships.html

Chapter 16: Stay Weird, Wedding Guests

Grubbs, J. B., & Exline, J. J. (2016). Trait entitlement: A cognitive-personality source of vulnerability to psychological distress. *Psychological Bulletin, 142*(11), 1204–1226. https://doi.org/10.1037/bul0000063

A Parting Word on Post-Wedding Feelings

The Big Wedding Planning Podcast (https://www.thebigweddingplanningpodcast.com/)

Interview with Jesse Kahn, LCSW-R, CST, an NYC-based psychotherapist and sex therapist and the Founder and Director at The Gender & Sexuality Therapy Center (https://gstherapycenter.com/)

Expert Bios

Trae Bodge

Trae Bodge is an accomplished lifestyle journalist and TV commentator who specializes in smart shopping and saving money. She has appeared on-air hundreds of times, including GMA3, NBC Nightly News, Inside Edition, and network affiliates around the country. Trae's expert commentary can be found on MSN.com, Millie magazine, Grow for CNBC, and elsewhere. You can find her money-saving tips at truetrae.com and @truetrae on Facebook, Instagram, and Twitter. Trae is also co-founder of OneTake, a media coaching firm.

Shirin Eskandani

Shirin is a life coach, public speaker, and writer who specializes in mindfulness and mindset work. She has been a featured wellness expert on the Today Show and in Shape and Cosmopolitan Magazine. Prior to building her successful coaching business, she was an award-winning opera singer, performing at Carnegie Hall and The Metropolitan Opera. Certified by the International Coach Federation, Shirin's holistic approach to transformation is influenced by her background in meditation, spirituality, and the arts. An inspiring and dynamic speaker, Shirin has presented at ALT Summit, Ignite Women Summit, Well Summit, Heal Haus, and the Assemblage. She is the co-founder of The Glow Up and Brown Girl Brunch and hosts two podcasts: Wholehearted Coaching: The Podcast and Two Girls Talking Shit. Learn more about Shirin's work at wholehearted-coaching.com.

Callie Exas

Callie Exas, MPH, MS, RDN, CPT, is a women's health and nutrition expert. As a Registered Dietitian Nutritionist & NASM Certified Personal Trainer, it is her mission to help women feel empowered in their bodies. In her practice, Callie takes a holistic look into the biological, physiological, and psychological components of her client's nutrition and self-care practices in order to heal their mind-body connection by addressing the impact of burnout on hormonal and metabolic function. Health and well-being are nuanced. It all begins by taking an individualized, evidence-based approach to nutrition and lifestyle factors at the root of any imbalance. While the journey is never linear, Callie guides her clients to help them better understand how to work with their bodies in order to feel energetic, confident, and resilient from the inside out. Connect with Callie online at www.callieexas.com or on Instagram at @womanup.wellness.

Jesse Kahn

Jesse Kahn LCSW-R, CST is the Founder, Director and a Sex Therapist at the Gender & Sexuality Therapy Center (G&STC), a New York City-based group of psychotherapists specializing in gender, sexuality, sex, and relationships. Prior to founding G&STC, Jesse graduated from Hunter College's Silberman School of Social Work, obtained their AASECT sex therapy certification, and studied and worked for The Karen Horney Clinic at The American Institute of Psychoanalysis, Center for Urban Community Services, Gay Men's Health Crisis (GMHC), and Housing Works. Learn more about the Gender & Sexuality Therapy Center at gstherapycenter.com.

Petronella Lugemwa

Petronella Lugemwa is a storyteller, speaker, educator, and Creative Director at Petronella Photography, an award-winning destination wedding and family photography studio based out of the New York area that specializes in helping multicultural, interracial, interfaith couples celebrate their love in a modern way and believes that what makes you different makes you beautiful. Check out Petronella's work at bypetronella.com.

Meera Mohan-Graham

Meera is a QPOC wedding planning advocate, artist, and coach, who works directly with couples to help them navigate the emotional and interpersonal aspects of planning, keep connected throughout the planning process, and translate shared values into specific planning decisions. Meera's ability to guide couples through these topics merges her work as a personal coach with her former work as a documentary wedding photographer. Serving couples with complex identities and histories, she also draws from her personal experience as a queer woman of color in an intercultural and interracial relationship with a trans man, and as someone who has navigated the relics of intergenerational trauma. Though she no longer documents weddings, she still incorporates photography into her work with her couples through an intimate couple's session that she facilitates and documents in person as part of celebrating who they are. Learn more at www.MeeraGraham.com.

Made in United States
North Haven, CT
03 August 2022

22193339R00130